Praise for *Becoming a Sun*

"David Karchere's *Becoming a Sun* is a sun; it literally shone through my heart the moment I began to read it. It is the sun of light, love, the radiance of Source glowing through each of us. With this book we are able to feel the sun within us. It is always true, but often so hard to remember. I consider the poems within it to be vital gifts to all who are emerging today, guiding our world toward greater love and oneness."

~ Barbara Marx Hubbard ~
FOUNDATION FOR CONSCIOUS EVOLUTION

"This book is so well written. David is such a great teacher. Reading *Becoming a Sun* is like having him sitting right next to you, explaining things clearly, calmly and compassionately.

"This is some wonderful learning made easy."

~ Cliff Barry ~
FOUNDER, SHADOW WORK

"It is pretty safe to say that never before in modern times has the world needed David Karchere's insightful and uplifting reflection of the human spirit quite as much as it does right now. *Becoming a Sun* offers a new way of understanding how the light that shines within us all will also illuminate the path that lies ahead in life's wondrous journey. Simply put, *Becoming a Sun* is a warm-hearted gift to the reader, a proclamation of the very best that is humanly possible."

~ Paul Bassis ~
PRODUCER, THE ARISE MUSIC AND CAMPING FESTIVAL

"*Becoming a Sun* is an affirmation of the unlimited potential of humanity. In heart-felt poetry and lucid prose, David Karchere dispels the illusions that keep people separate. His words reconnect the reader with the Divine Essence and inner wisdom that lead to oneness. A__ ' ' shares a brilliant recipe for personal a_ _ d needs this book!"

Farrell ~
WOR   's TEAM

"Wonderful poet, author, workshop leader, composer, teacher, and much more, David Karchere is a man to meet, hear, appreciate, and now READ. Having always deeply valued his inspirational talks and poetry, I am delighted to know I can now find them both in one place and share these with many friends. *Becoming a Sun* is all about how to provide a crucial difference in the world and the book may just be that crucial difference in your own life. At a time when many people are feeling defeated, here is a way to know personal victory."

~ **Dr. Tom Cooper** ~
Co-publisher, *MEDIA ETHICS* magazine
Professor, Emerson College

"I am so glad to endorse this book! Being born and having lived on the African Continent all my life, I know the fire and powerful influence of the Sun—the life-giving outer Sun. David Karchere's book, *Becoming a Sun*, invites all people to become Sun builders, by igniting the inner Sun that lives within the core of ourselves. I know that I carry that fire inside me.

"What is contained in David's book is a compelling and powerful invitation issued at this crucial time on our planet. Civilizations have come and gone, and despite all the new technological advances, we are still in dire need of a radical and powerful transformation to restore our world to its natural life-giving order. I believe that this book provides an assured map for those interested in unlocking primal knowledge in bringing our natural gifts of 'warmth, light and gravitas' to each other, and beyond us into the natural world."

~ **Anne-Lise Bure** ~
Managing Director, The Novalis Ubuntu Institute

"I have long admired David Karchere's genuine nature and his sincerity and passion as a spiritual director. *Becoming a Sun* is a glowing book about the beautiful essence and potential for life contributions that reside within each of us. Reading it will surely inspire you to radiate your unique gifts."

~ **Jim Sharon, Ed.D.** ~
Psychologist, author and Coach for Soulful Couples

"David nailed it in this book. Becoming the Sun is a growth and transformation process we ALL go through in life. We all are made to shine and this book provides a beautiful combination of poetic inspiration, metaphorical enchantment, sound advice and a beautiful philosophy to live from. Bravo David Karchere. Thank you for bringing this work to the world."

~ **George Carroll** ~

Changing the World, One Audience at a Time

"For 30 years, David Karchere has been for me a close friend, mentor and musical collaborator. In that time, I've seen him uplift and inspire thousands with his message of personal and collective potential—through his speaking, live programs, writing, coaching and music. In *Becoming a Sun*, David puts the earned wisdom of his own personal transformation, and his deeply considered perspective of what is most needed in our world today, into potent, clear words that call those with ears to hear to stand in their innate radiance. For us, you and I, and our world, it is our destiny to become a sun—a brightly radiant and creative expression of Being. This book, in a heartful and bold way, shows the way. I am deeply thankful that these ideas, and the enlivening spirit that gave them birth, are in the world today at this remarkable time of awakening. There are few books I can honestly say that everyone with a burning desire to manifest their great potential for positive contribution must read. This is one of them."

~ **Dr. Michael Gaeta** ~

Acupuncturist, Nutritionist and Educator

"Though one's spiritual practice can be a solitary endeavor, David knows—and all of us eventually realize—that it takes us on a journey to serve fully for the good of all. This journey takes courage as each one of us has to embrace who we truly are and step into the life that is calling us. David's book, *Becoming a Sun*, is a clear and compassionate companion for anyone needing support as they pursue this awakening. I highly recommend it."

~ **Sarah McLean** ~

Director, Meditation Teacher Academy

"At the core of this book is the simple yet potent assertion that the world we experience is itself the product of our collective consciousness. Especially now, as global crises compound, this insight into our most fundamental creative capacities sheds a radiant light on the road ahead, providing valuable guidance on how to let our own suns shine."

~ **Emanuel Kuntzelman** ~

PRESIDENT, GREENHEART INTERNATIONAL

Becoming

A

Sun

Emotional and Spiritual Intelligence for a Happy and Fulfilling Life

David Karchere

Becoming a Sun

Emotional and Spiritual Intelligence for a Happy and Fulfilling Life

ISBN: 978-1-798436-45-5 (paperback)

For more information, please write:
Best Seller Publishing®
1346 Walnut Street, #205
Pasadena, CA 91106
or call 1 (626) 765-9750
Toll Free: 1(844) 850-3500
Visit us online at: www.BestSellerPublishing.org

Printed in the United States of America.

Dedication

To awakening people everywhere

Contents

PREFACE

*The earth has received the embrace of the sun and
we shall see the results of that love.*

~ SITTING BULL ~

When I entered Staples High School in 1968, the Vietnam War was
raging. Friends came back to my hometown of Westport, Connecticut,
from the Democratic Convention in Chicago, Illinois, having witnessed
heads bashed and bruised by Mayor Richard J. Daley's police. We quickly
set up a symposium at the high school that featured clergyman and peace
activist William Sloane Coffin as a part of our protest of the war.

With my girlfriend, Rachel, I became interested in *alternative
community*, a theme that has pervaded my life since. We made plans to
live and work at Kibbutz Mishmarot and travel through Israel in the
summer of 1969. My parents were going to help fund the trip. But in
March, the tension between my father and me became so great that he
told me to leave home. Uwe Moeller, the German chef at the restaurant
where I worked, took me in. I earned the money to travel to Israel with
the hope of finding my dream—a community of people who were
committed to creating a new world. If I found it, I expected to emigrate.

I spent my days in Israel moving irrigation pipes in the cotton fields
with a crew from many nations. Dovi, the kibbutznik who led the crew,
called out "one, two, three" for the lifting of the set of pipes in Hebrew,

"Eh'ad, shnyim, shlosha!" Walking around the main campus later with my Polish friend, Edmond, we were at a loss for how to greet each other. He didn't speak English and I certainly didn't speak Polish. Our greeting became "Eh'ad, shnyim, shlosha!"

Rachel and I had fabulous adventures, but Israel did not have what I was looking for.

When we returned to Westport, my parents picked me up at JFK International Airport, and without saying hardly a word about it, they took me home. I was shocked to see the decay in the culture in which I had been living. My friends had been to the Woodstock music festival and had become even more involved in drugs than before. And the horror of Vietnam continued, with young men only a little older than me dying by the thousands.

In October 1969, with friends, I organized a march of 1,200 people from the high school to downtown, where there was a rally with several thousand more joining us. I was a speaker at the rally, proclaiming "Peace now!" and denouncing the injustice of the war. With our numbers growing, the next month we organized buses to Washington, DC, to protest on the National Mall.

Through this period, I became more and more desolate. I was horrified by what I saw happening in the world around me. And I was searching desperately for an answer—for the world, and for my own life. I began to see a psychiatrist, to understand my own angst, and to explore psychiatry for the answer I was looking for. It didn't help.

In the winter of 1969–70, with Rachel and my best friend, Will Carpenter, and three other friends, I hatched a plan to start a commune. We each began earning our share of the purchase price for the real estate and organized trips to look at available farm properties. We found 163 acres of land in Canaan, Maine, with the shell of a cabin on it. It cost $5,000. When school ended, we packed our things and headed to Maine. My commitment to myself was that I would let go of all the concerns that were plaguing my heart. I told myself to let go and open to a new experience.

It was a magnificent summer, with a shimmering sky full of the Northern Lights, skinny-dipping in Lake George, smoking grass, and enjoying passionate conversation. By the end of the summer, all my friends had left but Rachel. And by October it was getting cold and we had totally run out of money. We returned to Westport, funded by an Indian head penny we sold for $5. Staples accepted me back and I completed my final year of high school.

But while I was in Maine, I had encountered the writings of Martin Cecil. I read booklets with such titles as *The Fountain of Life, The Longing of Your Heart, and The Worth of Work*. In September 1971, after graduating from high school, I attended a one-month class in aware, spiritual living, where Martin taught the last two weeks of the program. It was held at Lake Rest Hotel, which was located in the Shandelee, New York, area of the Catskill Mountains at the highest point in Sullivan County. While I was there, the fall colors peaked. The mountains burst into flame in shades of yellow, red, and orange from the maple trees.

At 18 years old, I was the youngest person in the program. At a personal level, the gap between me and Martin could not have been wider. He was 62 years old at the time, more than three times my age. He came from a noble family in England, and when referred to by his English title he was known as Lord Martin Cecil. By the time I met him, he had been offering spiritual teaching for about 30 years while leading the community of 100 Mile House in the South Cariboo region of interior British Columbia.

I was just beginning to open up spiritually. I soaked in the teachings. They answered the deepest questions of my heart and offered inspiration and hope for the world and for my own life. I felt waves of peace flood through my being as Martin spoke.

The last session of the class was on a Friday morning. I have little memory of the subject. But the experience of it changed my life.

Verbal descriptions of spiritual experiences cannot capture the wonder of them. I have no words large enough or rich enough to communicate the vision that came to me. It was not a physical vision. But, nonetheless, it was as lucid and as real as anything I have seen with my physical eyes. The best description I have for it is that it was of a heavenly court. Not angels exactly as we think of them. But heavenly Beings with light emanating from them and all around. And in the midst of them all, there was a Being of the most exquisite, overwhelming love.

For me, the sun had come out from behind the clouds. Everything in me turned molten. I was in awe. When the session concluded, I stumbled out the side door that led directly outside. I got far enough away from everyone else, walked into a stand of small trees and shrubs, and sobbed.

I cannot believe the sacredness of what I have just seen.

I understand now that I received the seed of grace in those moments, and it changed me. That seed has stayed with me from that day to this. Through a lot of joy and through times that have seemed incredibly hard, that grace has been with me. It has led me on my way with its light, its gravity, and its warmth. The knowing of it has grown and deepened through my life.

Grace comes in a unique way to every person. This was how it came to me.

Since that day, I've devoted my life to nurturing the seed that was planted in me and sharing it with others. I've had the opportunity to serve and lead a global spiritual community and facilitate experiences of grace through speaking, workshops, and developing community.

And over the years, I've come to see that the journey of grace is actually the journey of becoming a sun. Our world needs the radiance of grace, the warmth of blessing, and the gravity of courage, and it's up to us to become a sun and do what many of us have been called to do since we were young . . . to create a new world.

ACKNOWLEDGMENTS

I believe it is impossible to create anything of value without the help of others. Certainly, that is true for this book. *Becoming a Sun* reflects a lifetime of learning, so there are many, many people who have contributed to it. Thanks to you all. I offer my gratitude to the following people by name.

To Loved Ones . . .

To Joyce and Helena. They have been with me on my path, and they loved and supported me when it seemed like the world was falling apart. I cannot imagine two more beautiful women, each walking their own path.

To Al and Ginny, who loved me, challenged me, and gave me their wisdom, courage, and determination.

To Martha, Peter, and Sarah. Thank you for understanding me.

To People Who Inspired Me . . .

To Lloyd Arthur Meeker, for his remarkable vision and enlightened teachings.

To Yienan Song, who showed me an enlightened vision of the arts.

To Cliff Barry, for his remarkable work with the emotional body, and for coaching me at a critical time in my life.

To Dr. Bill Bahan, whom I met in 1969 as a young man of the Sixties looking for an answer. His suit and Coke-bottle glasses made me think he was one of the squarest people I had ever met. Then his humor and his vision saved my life.

To Martin Cecil, the finest man I have ever known.

To the Book Team . . .

To Shareen Ewing, who has been my editor for many years, and who did all the initial editing of this book. Thank you for believing in me as an author and for sharing my passion for the vision that inspired the book.

To Amanda Johnson of True To Intention, for her great insight and expertise in coaching me on a revision of the book.

To my illustrator, Diana Bychkova, whose wonderful imagination presented the message of the book in visual form.

To My Community . . .

To Jane Anetrini, a woman of simple and profound commitment. Thank you for seeing my leadership, supporting it, and for leading and teaching with me.

To my Sunrise Ranch community, for becoming a sun.

To friends around the world.

To the Source of All . . .

I am inspired every day by a reality I cannot see and cannot adequately name. Call it angels, call it God, or call it heaven. How do you say thank you to the source of life? To the source of wisdom? Love? And all possibility? Thank you.

INTRODUCTION

*Awareness is like the sun. When it shines
on things, they are transformed.*

~ THICH NHAT HANH ~

It is our personal and collective destiny to become a sun—to become on the outside what we already are on the inside: a conscious presence of Universal Love. This destiny is behind everything we experience as human beings, however we interpret it—every passion, every adventure, every challenge, even what might look like terrible setbacks in our life. Through it all, the core of who we are as a being of Universal Love is shucking off the unnatural limitations that we, as human beings, tend to accept for ourselves. That core within us seeks to shine freely through us, as us, into the world.

This book tracks the universal process by which we become a sun. It shows the amazing ways that the core of Universal Love creates a whole human being who is capable of carrying the full radiance of who we are into the world. In the seven chapters of the book, I depict, through poetry and prose, how a person is initiated into seven experiences on this journey:

The Warmth of Blessing

The Atmosphere of Understanding

The Bursts of Action

The Fusion of Fulfilling Mission

The Rays of Enlightened Thought

The Gravity of Courage

The Radiance and Reflections of Grace

When fully embraced by the person, these experiences become virtues of life expression. Each chapter of the book is devoted to one of these virtues.

My premise is this: The difference between a joyful, fulfilling life and an unhappy, unfulfilled life is conscious awareness and understanding. When people understand that their personal destiny is to become a sun, and they understand the process by which that becomes a reality, they embrace the experience. They become a conscious participant in their own destiny. Without that awareness and understanding, they are fighting that destiny. They feel threatened by the powerful creative urge within themselves to become all they are meant to be, and all they long to experience.

At a collective level, humanity is experiencing a great shift. We are participating in a great leap forward in the evolution of consciousness that is taking us from an experience that is defined by what is affecting us from the outside world to creating our own experience as human beings. Up to this point, humanity has largely believed that it was at the mercy of forces outside itself. It is becoming increasingly clear that it is we, ourselves, who are impacting the world more than the other way around, and that as humanity we are receiving the impact of our own creation.

So while we used to think that the manifest reality in our world was determining our conscious experience, the awareness is dawning that what is unfolding in our conscious experience is creating our manifest reality. This is happening at a global level for humankind as a whole. Global warming is one of the more obvious examples of human impact on the planet. The erosion of the ozone layer, and the twin threats of nuclear war and the meltdown of nuclear power plants have forced an acknowledgment of humankind's power to wreak destruction at a global level.

Through the ages, scientific discovery has changed human understanding of the world and its own place in that world. Astronomer Nicolaus Copernicus, physicist Galileo Galilei, and scientist Sir Isaac Newton upset the Judeo–Christian worldview that prevailed in their era. Fossil fuel technology and mass production launched humankind into the Industrial Age. Now, nuclear technology has launched us into the Atomic Age, and quantum physics has challenged our fundamental understanding of the relationship between consciousness and the manifest world, showing that the presence of consciousness changes the behavior of creation.

There is a growing body of scientific knowledge that is documenting the power of consciousness. I salute the work of author Lynne McTaggart, who has documented some of this research and is doing her own research into the power of intention. The HeartMath Institute has collated and presented research showing that the physical heart and the emotional realm are significant factors in the human experience.

Dr. Larry Dossey has documented the role that prayer plays in healing. Now there are many people and groups who are making it clear that human consciousness is a critical factor in the human experience, and many are also teaching how to let consciousness shift so that what manifests in form might change.

As this work continues, and as human consciousness continues to evolve, I believe we will come to see the current scientific documentation of the impact of consciousness to be the beginning of the awareness that the whole human world is being created by the state of consciousness of humanity.

Scientific research approaches these issues from the outside looking in. It measures the observable phenomena and postulates that changes in consciousness might have created those phenomena. That is vital work. And still, in the living of life, we each necessarily live from the inside looking out. If our consciousness were the vehicle we drive through life, we would not drive that vehicle from outside of it, looking into the vehicle. We live within the vehicle of consciousness, looking out through it to our world. We drive the vehicle from within it, not as if we were outside it with a remote control. So this book is written from that perspective. It depicts the vehicle of consciousness as seen from the inside and offers insights on how consciousness can shift and develop from that perspective.

Our world needs this understanding. As the human race faces the opportunities and perils of the 21st century, including financial crisis, terrorism, global warming, and a world population that has tripled in the life of the Baby Boomer generation, there is a simple, yet frightening awareness that is surfacing within humanity as a whole—collective human consciousness has the power of creation within it, for better or for worse. And that creative power is accessed individually as a person moves out of the experience of being victimized by the world around him or her to an experience of personal empowerment.

But for individuals to experience a change personally, they have to do something about their own personal, conscious evolution. They have to understand how the processes of consciousness work to manifest a world of form, and choose to let those processes work differently than they have for the mass of humanity up to this point. As that understanding develops, individuals have the opportunity to become people of influence at the global level and play a part in conscious evolution of humanity as a whole. They have the opportunity to become a sun—a conscious focus for the power of creation in the world.

This book is about that journey. It is about finding in ourselves, and in other people, the creative mechanisms of consciousness. This is hard work. You can't see, with your physical eyes, the various parts of yourself and others that form the mechanisms of consciousness. And if you can't see them, it is hard to know how those mechanisms work together to create a world. Yet we know they do.

Life is different from one person to the next, largely based on the individuals' mastery of the creative factors intrinsic to their own thoughts and feelings. So this book is an in-depth exploration of the parts of ourselves, and of all people, that create consciousness and create a world. It names the hidden gateways in human experience for the power of consciousness and brings awareness of the wisdom required for the creative use of that power.

The ancients used the four elements—water, air, earth, and fire—to symbolize the most essential forces at work in the creative process and in the human experience. Sacred texts passed down over millennia, in both the East and the West, contain keys to how these elements are accessible to us as human beings, and how we play a part in creation. Hinduism, Buddhism, Greek philosopher Aristotle, and the ancient Babylonians all refer to the four elements. In the Bible book of Genesis, the spirit of God moves on the face of the *waters*. The *waters* are gathered together under the heaven (*air*). And the dry land (*earth*) emerges. And on the fourth day, the sun (*fire*) appears.

Today's psychology, science, and religion have other ways of describing how creation occurs, and that understanding has done much to dispel the ignorance and suspicion that still pervade so much of human thinking. Yet there is an understanding available through the use of this ancient naming of creation that is not available otherwise. It is an aspect of the symbol and poetry that is the language of the human soul.

I have thought long and hard about how I might convey the truth that I have sought to share in this book. There are approaches I tried to take to my writing that were more intellectually precise, but less understandable to the way the human soul understands the process of creation at its depth. So the chapters of the book are designed to be a guide to the creative process through the language of the soul.

Nonetheless, poetry and metaphor, of itself, is not the point of this book. At their best, words track an experience and convey information that can't be fully captured in words. My hope is that what is happening inside us all is invoked more fully for me in the sharing of this book, and for you as you read it. These words are my best attempt to represent the message I receive on the inside, sometimes in words, but most often through feeling and experience; an inner pulse and vibration that creates music in my ears and pictures in my mind. The words of this book share the voice of the creation compulsion that speaks with me. My hope is that you share that experience for yourself as you read.

In each chapter of the book, I've also included a personal story of being initiated into the seven experiences of becoming a sun in hopes that the ideas of the book will become more relatable and real for you. I trust that you understand that your initiation into becoming a sun is unfolding in a way that is unique to you and your life.

As you begin your journey through this book, I want to encourage you to remember that the creative process is not a linear process. You might find yourself revisiting the experiences of blessing described in Chapter One more times than you think possible, and the same applies to all the chapters of the book. If you are like many of those who previewed the book, you will actually feel the warmth of the sun within and around you as you read through some chapters; and you'll feel the cold and isolation that often is felt when the sun seems to have been covered by a cloud. Just trust that as you revisit these places within you, you are making progress, and you keep moving forward.

For the most part, I have spoken in the second person, addressing my words to "you." This is as close as I can come to how I address the matters raised in this book in my own personal process, as I carry on my own inner dialogue. It also seems the most direct way to address you, the reader. In everyday speech, I might couch what I say as my vision, or my understanding of things, or my experience. In writing, I think that would be tedious. Here, in this introduction, I invite you to consider as you read what is presented in this book as my experience and understanding, and to ponder whether or not it is true for you.

This book is designed to be an operator's guide to the evolution of human consciousness. Because consciousness is composed of both thought and feeling, I have set forth both a mental model of consciousness and a map for intuitive understanding of the emotional elements of consciousness. So the book is meant to be understood at the level of emotion and intuition as well as at the level of the mind. I believe that the emotional realm is where the most profound changes take place. What happens there equips us to lead a fulfilling life and to assist others to do the same. Emotional mastery sets us up to be mentally wise, physically healthy, and spiritually awake.

While this book could be read cover to cover, I recommend that you read it a chapter at a time. I picture it sitting on someone's night table, being read before the person goes to sleep. I have written the book in the rhythms of speech, so it is meant to be read in that rhythm. I doubt you will gain much from the book by skimming through it for the important ideas, even though the ideas that inform this book are at the foundation of the human experience.

Again, it's not linear, and it's not meant to be. It might frustrate you because your linear brain is always looking for the answer . . . the steps . . . the process. But this is about the creative process the soul experiences as it becomes a sun. And the experience of the process is different for everyone.

So, you might really love one chapter and resonate with it, and then be totally annoyed by the next chapter. You might feel frustrated, confused, even angry through certain parts of this book because it is designed to speak to your heart and soul, not just your mind.

When you start to feel those emotions—breathe, journal, take a walk/ break, and then allow yourself to be drawn back into the book, called by it. Remember, the book is designed to lead you to the transformational map that is already present within your own heart. Keep reading with faith that your soul is being nourished with something that it needs.

I believe that the truth behind the words of this book is relevant to every aspect of human experience, from the most intimate areas of love and family, to the fields of business, organizational leadership, and finance. Of course, you will have to see how it applies to you and your life destiny. As you read, I invite you to consider how the essential ideas of this book are relevant to all facets of your life.

I understand that, for most people, the idea that there could be a shift in consciousness or a change of heart for all humanity that would answer the most pressing issues of our day might seem unlikely. Nonetheless, that shift and change is already occurring in people around the globe. Like any significant shift in human paradigms, it is beginning with a relatively small number of people. If you are one of them, congratulations! You are probably in the midst of a fulfilling, sometimes perilous adventure—a learning experience of the highest order. So if you have chosen to take an active part in the evolution of consciousness, I wish you well, and I hope the words that follow assist you on that journey.

You are becoming a sun.

Chapter One

The Warmth
of
Blessing

*To love and be loved is to feel the
sun from both sides.*

~ David Viscott ~

Being a Sun

What your world, and the people in it, need most from you is for you to
be a sun.

They need your warmth. Your ability to offer your care for their well-
being. Your ability to offer blessing. Nothing imposed. Nothing affected.
Just the abiding spirit of love, constant in your heart of hearts.

When faced with the coldness of other people, or the coldness of the
world, return that coldness with your warmth. And in the fire that fuels
your warmth, transform what the world gives to you without reaction.
Let the coldness be transformed and transmuted in your inner fire until
it is burnt to ash and ascending flame. Then return the fire of your love
to your world. Let your world feel the warmth of the sun through you.

Your world needs your light. Your wisdom. Your intelligence. Your vision. You have the ability to light up your world so that the people in it can see. Faced with judgment or condemnation. Faced with prejudice and bias. Or faced with the dogged determination to imagine the worst thing that could happen and act out of fear of that. Bring your light. Not in others' faces. Not as a bludgeon. Use your light to illuminate the path ahead. The light that illuminates not only what is but what could be if we would only let it. This is the light that lets humanity find its way.

Your world and the people in it need your light even more than they need your warmth. Your light is the eternal, shining truth you know in your bones. Never imposed, but made freely available wherever you are. Let your world see because of the light of the sun through you.

Your world needs the gravity you bring that holds the flow of creation in its orbit. This is your capacity to hold people in whatever process they are in. This is that attractive power that moves through you, which brings people close to your fire when they need to be.

The gravity you bring to your world is born out of your stability as a sun. Your acceptance of your rightful place in the heavens and your refusal to move from that place. Because you abide where you belong, you draw to you the people, the circumstances, the physical substance, and the financial substance that is longing to come to you and play a part in your world.

Your gravity is also that force that holds you together. It brings all the parts of who you are to one place to participate in your burning and your light.

Let your world feel the gravity of what is happening in you. Let all who inhabit your world find their rightful orbit. Let them come together in your solar system because of the gravity of the sun you bring.

As you are a sun—as you bring the warmth, the light, and the gravity that is yours to bring—you offer orientation to your world and the people who inhabit it. Even as travelers find the four directions by the position of the sun in the sky, your world needs you to be a point of reference. People in your world want to know that a human life could be miraculous. Creative! Fulfilling! Full of real pleasure! As people have relied on the stars, or on the sun itself, to find their way, let your world find the point of orientation you bring when you are being a sun.

What your world and the people in it need most from you is for you to be a sun. It is the most natural thing for you to do to bring your warmth, your light, and the gravity of who you are. And when you do, you provide a point of orientation for your world. Any shortcomings or limitations you believe you have don't stop you from being a sun. And as you are a sun in your world, any shortcomings and limitations have a way of being transformed and transmuted. They do not stop you from being a sun.

Everyone's world needs them to be a sun. If you and I have both awakened to this greatest of needs, we can become aware of each other. We can become aware that there are people around the world who have awakened to the reality that they are born to be suns. In fact, we are born to build One Sun. Not just a sun for your world. Not just a sun for my world. One Sun for THE world. Are you ready to be a Sun builder? The world needs such a Sun.

Every time people have come together for this grand task, there has been friction among them. People resist their own calling to be a sun. They fight with other people who have that same calling. As the gravity of the One Sun calls us together, there is always friction. Expect it! As Sun builders, our job is to transform friction to fusion. Let the gravity of the One Sun that brings us together bring fusion. With the warmth of the Sun. With the light of the Sun. With each other, so that together we may be One Sun. On earth! Within the body of humanity. That transforming power! That gravity!

Let us build a sun.

Even if you didn't call it Becoming a Sun, when did you start your journey?

The Sun for Your Creative Field

You find yourself at the center of a field of awareness. In that field, there are worlds within worlds, overlapping, and interrelating, all composing the one field of awareness with you at the center. Copernicus discovered that the sun, not the Earth, is the center of our solar system. Yet while the sun is at the center of the solar system, you are at the center of the system around you. Your field extends in all directions around you, out to infinity.

Closest to you are your own thoughts and feelings and your own physical awareness. Moving through this inmost aspect of your creative field is your own life energy—your spirit—ebbing and flowing through thought and feeling and through your physical body. You have the remarkable ability to change how your energy flows by opening up new levels of awareness in your thoughts and feelings. No doubt you have experimented with that ability, noticing how you experience life energy differently, depending on what you choose to think and say and do. This immediate creative field of thought, feeling, and physical experience responds to you as you become more conscious of it. But if you want to gain that awareness, you cannot be identified with this closest dimension of your creative field. You cannot act as if you are what you think and feel.

You are a sun for your own capacities, which are designed to be filled with your own sun substance—your warmth, your light, your gravity—radiating from the reality of who you are. In the radiance of the sun, who you are, your body, mind, and emotional realm thrive.

In the stellar nursery, where you are developing as a sun, experiment. Change the way you enfold your own human capacities. Change the energy that you move through your capacities. Invite yourself to experience something different. Challenge yourself. Forgive yourself. See what happens. Find out how different your life is as you are a sun.

Your creative field extends at least as far as your present awareness. It includes the people who are close to you in your life, and the people further away. To other people, it might seem that you are in their creative field, and for them that is true. But for you, all these people are in your world of awareness. You are the sun for them, and they are orbiting in your solar system. They are in your creative field, and they respond differently according to the energy that is emanating through you. And your energetic emanation changes, depending on what you do with your consciousness.

Most people do not have the awareness that they are a sun, so they do not have an awareness of what their energetic emanation is creating in their field. There is a trick of the mind that is almost universal in people, hiding this awareness. People think that their creative field—their body, their mind, their feelings, and the people and circumstances of their world—is causing their experience. And they believe they are being forced to express themselves the way they are by powers outside themselves. They believe that their field is causing them to feel what they are feeling, to think what they are thinking, and to speak and act the way they do.

When a person becomes aware that they are a sun, they realize that they have a choice. They do not have to be a slave to their own reaction to their creative field. They don't have to alter their radiance based on what other people say or do. They don't have to alter their radiance based on how they feel themselves. The sun can always shine. When a person awakens to this, they begin to notice all the ways they have tended to alter their radiance. They notice how they have created disturbance in their creative field, based on their reaction to it. They might have acted out in anger, withdrawn, become depressed, and then reacted even more to that disturbance, creating a vicious cycle.

It can be hard to face the way your personal reactions have caused destruction in your field. But because you are a sun, you are becoming more and more aware of your radiation and what it creates in the world.

And you are becoming more and more aware that your world thrives in your warmth, your light, and in your gravitational field.

This knowledge is the key to all leadership, at whatever level. It is the key for leaders of organizations, communities, families, and countries. It is the key for living a fulfilled life. It is the key to happiness.

What your world and the people in it need most from you is for you to be a sun.

Recall a time when you were being a sun. How did it feel?
Have you caught yourself choosing not to shine?
What happens for you when you make that choice?

Amidst the Wet Falling Snow in Nagano

In 1999, I was in Tokyo, Japan, on business. Yukio, a man who was introduced to me by mutual friends, invited me to meet with four people in Nagano, once the site of the Winter Olympics. Yukio is a professional translator. It was my first trip to Japan; in fact, my first trip to Asia. I was amazed and fascinated by the Japanese people.

After an intense week of business negotiations, I headed alone to the Tokyo train station on Friday afternoon where Yukio found me. It was not hard. I was one of the few Americans on the platform. He was slightly built with a kind smile and understanding eyes. We got on the bullet train for the two-hour ride to Nagano.

Before the train reached the outskirts of Tokyo, Yukio told me—with a lot of excitement—that he had managed to organize about 25 people to join us at the home of his friend, Jin. They were eager to participate in a weekend workshop in spirituality, offered by me! And even though most of them did not speak English, he would be happy to translate.

Amazing! Totally unplanned! But what an opportunity! Can I pull it off?

I told him I was looking forward to facilitating the workshop.

Later that evening in Nagano, the women enjoyed a bath together in the bath house that Jin had built on the property. Jin was a successful businessman in semiretirement. Also handy and capable, he had built a beautiful retreat center in the mountains. When they had finished, Yukio, Jin, and I—who were the only men who had yet arrived—took the waters ourselves. We walked through the snow, took off our shoes before entering, and enjoyed the steam and the smell of cedar wood that lined the walls.

I've never done this before! What a way to experience Japanese culture!
I feel like I am about to enter the inner sanctum of it.

In the course of our conversation (with Yukio's translation), we discovered that we were all born within a period of three weeks in 1953. All Aquarians!

I looked at my new friends and shared what was in my heart. "I believe that we three incarnated together for a reason. We must have a great spiritual mission that we share, which is coming to focus in our time together this weekend." They all nodded their heads in quiet agreement before I finished. "I am really looking forward to seeing what happens this weekend. And if this workshop is going to be a success, I will really need your help." My heart began to race with excitement for the experience ahead.

The meeting space was on the second floor of the retreat building, a rectangle with four glass walls between wooden beams, overlooking the wet, snow-covered trees.

There was a Japanese woman who was seen as an elder by the group. To begin the workshop, she and I smudged each of the participants with incense after they ascended the stairs and entered the room.

I taught all morning with Yukio translating. He was so conscientious! At a critical juncture, he stopped, deep in thought. "Hmmm," he wondered out loud, laughed, and then did his best to explain the meaning of my words.

There is a cliché about people from Asia that their thoughts and feelings are inscrutable for Westerners. That was certainly how it felt to me that morning. Everyone listened attentively. Dutifully, it seemed to me. But I kept wondering, *Are they understanding me? Agreeing with me? Experiencing anything meaningful?*

At a break in the afternoon, I pulled Yukio and Jin aside. "You guys have to tell me how I'm doing. Am I getting through to this group? Do they understand what I am presenting? Is it resonating with them?"

Yukio translated for Jin, and, in a kindly way, they reassured me that the workshop was going well and I should stay with what I was doing.

I pressed on. More stoic faces. If there was something moving at depth, they were not going to show it to me, a foreigner, or so it seemed.

Later that afternoon, I thought I saw a tear rolling down the cheek of a young woman, out of the corner of her eye.

Was that really a tear? What is that about? What is happening?

The next morning was magical. There was a wet snow falling. Big, fat snowflakes outside all four glass walls. We entered a group dialogue, sharing our own process of healing and spiritual emergence. As I listened to the personal stories and looked at the faces around the room, I saw more tears. First, just one or two. As the session continued, I realized that I was in the middle of a full-scale meltdown of the heart. It had become an impromptu community of deep love, and, in the middle of that love, their hearts were exposed, and they were healing. They were loving one another into wholeness, and they were letting me in. I was a part of that community. I was not a foreigner. I was on the inside of the community looking out, even as I was looking out of the glass windows at the wet snow. Not only that. I had played a part in creating that crucible of love. I had brought the fire of that love, and they had trusted it. My own heart warmed and melted a little more as I listened to each of their stories.

To end our sessions, the Japanese elder and I greeted people as they exited down the stairs. First me, then her. I spoke these words in English, and then she spoke the same words in Japanese. "You are a being of remarkable love with a wonderful gift to bring to the world." Simple words. They soaked into these people's hearts like water on the Arizona desert.

There was one man of about 30 who had shared a painful story of his relationship with his father. He had bleached blond hair, and through the entire workshop he was stone-faced. It was clear to me that he had a hurting heart. As he approached me, about 15 feet away, his knees buckled. He stumbled up to me, wrapping his arms around me, clutching me like he would never let go, and sobbed. He muttered his appreciation in Japanese, looking into my eyes until he was ready to go.

Love to the heart. The dynamic is so simple. So primal. At the root of everything that has any meaning in our life. We have love to bring and love to receive. And when we are initiated into that dynamic, it is hard to know who is giving and who is receiving. For my Japanese friends on that day, they received love to the heart. So did I. And we all had the opportunity to give it. But someone has to be courageous enough to initiate that experience. That weekend in Japan, I had the privilege of being that someone.

The Waters of the Creative Field

Just as the sun of our solar system activates all the elements of Planet Earth, the fire of fusion in you has a profound effect on the elements of your world. As it heats the oceans of the world, sets the winds in motion, and warms the earth, the sun makes all forms of life possible on Earth and sustains those life-forms through its radiance. When you are bringing your radiance to your creative field, that field is profoundly affected by you. The waters of your soul are warmed. The atmosphere you share with other people is different. Your creative field comes to life in your radiance, and new forms of life spring up around you—new opportunities, new friendships, and a quickening that makes what is already happening in your life feel new.

What first occurs when the sun comes out in your experience is that your emotional body basks in its radiance—the waters of your soul are warmed. The emotional body loves to feel our warmth. It loves to receive warmth from your own source or from someone else. The radiance of the sun that we bring is the power of love, and whenever love is received by the waters of our soul, we feel a blessing that nourishes us like nothing else. In some respects, it does not seem to matter how love is received in the emotional body. Whether it seems to be from another person, from within, or from the eternal reality beyond space and time, blessing—a deep spirit of love and care—is given and received. And the deeper the fire of love enters the waters of our emotional body, the more powerful the impact.

Can you feel how your emotional body responds when you expose it to the warmth of love? Think of a time in your life when you felt the radiance of love from another person. Call to mind how you felt when you were held in a loving way by someone precious to you.

Most people are starved for this kind of experience. In the beginning of a romantic relationship, people open to this kind of deep interchange. But all too often they go on to what they see as more important concerns. They forget they are a sun. They fall into an experience of reaction to the other person and the world around them and become unconscious of what they are creating in their relationship.

Sometimes people feel profound blessing from the Divine in their life. They feel blessed by a higher power, however they name it. In the experience of deep prayer—which does not have to be in a religious surrounding—people might feel the fire of the sun. They might know that they are profoundly loved. But this blessing will eventually leave their experience if they are not willing to be a sun themselves for their creative field.

The relationship between the fire of love and the deep water of emotion is one of six primary relationships in your creative field. The relationship between fire and water creates the experience of blessing and of being blessed. It is the beginning of all true romance.

In the materialistic world in which we live, this experience is often dismissed in favor of what are thought to be the more practical concerns in life. The results are disastrous. Most people are starving for the experience of blessing without knowing it. They are unaware of the craving of their waters for the blessing of the sun. No matter what might be accomplished in life, this inner craving can trouble a person. It can produce anger and depression. The lack of this blessing can show itself as negative blessing that comes out in a person's words and deeds—an expression that sends a chill to the feelings of other people.

Can you feel how much your waters crave the blessing of the sun? If you are in touch with that inner longing, you know something about the way the souls of all people crave the warmth of the sun. They long to feel acknowledgment, honor, appreciation, and loving compassion.

Your body is composed mostly of water, and the fluids of the body have a vital part to play in your emotional experience and in your physical health. When you are being a sun, you encourage those fluids to flow easily and in balance to where they are needed. You encourage your emotional flow, without constriction, when and where it is needed.

Your feelings can be an ally, not a liability, when you are being a sun. Their flow fuels your creative thought. And when your feelings flow through your words and your actions, you act with power in your world.

The icy parts of the waters of your soul melt under the influence of love. If there is ice, if there are frozen and hurt parts of you, they will thaw in the light of your sun so they can circulate once again. The spirit of blessing brings healing to the heart.

Your closest creative field, your human capacity, is made mostly of water, but so is the rest of your creative field. Most of the world is water. Watch what happens when the sun rises in you to shine on the oceans of your world. Watch what happens when you let blessing flow through you; when your words and actions carry radiance to other people. Not in arrogance or condescension. Not forcing yourself on other people. Just simple words and deeds that have your love behind them.

Your creative field is made mostly of water and, when that water thaws, it flows like a river and moves with the tides of the creative process. If you want to be a true and effective leader for your creative field, you must warm the waters of your world by allowing blessings to flow through you.

If you look at the people in your world and wonder why they are having a hard time, why they are living an unfulfilled life, why they are not living in creativity, think about this: They might be missing the warmth of the sun on their waters. And they might need you to help them feel that. Show compassion to your creative field. Give the warmth of your sun.

Think of the expression of blessing that would bring warmth to your emotional body.
Think of the words that could give voice to that blessing, and drink in the blessing of those words. You might even imagine a person who could speak those words to you.
Now think about how you could speak words like that to someone else who is open to it. Probably something short, without overdoing it.
Just enough to let them feel the blessing of the sun through you.

She Came That Morning

She came that morning,
her presence announced
by the candies on the Christmas tree,
and the smell of pine
from the boughs on the mantle;
by the feel of something
that had never been in the house before,
as if the hard corners of the woodwork had softened,
and the walls themselves had relaxed.

Things changed after she moved in.
There was less time
for Ludlum novels,
for worrying about the world,
or for the making of small things.
There was much that was so important
but which gave way to walks in splendid gardens,
and moonlit strolls on a smooth-pebbled beach;
to playgrounds lined with the tallest buildings,
and canoe rides cheered on by deer on the river's banks.

The world changed when they were together,
as if there was no hurt so deep,
no injustice so great,
that it could not be healed in the cradle of their love,
made right by long walks in the company of hooting owls,
and by the melodies that wove among their hearts.
Such was the nature of the love
that had called them together
and ran between them in rivers and streams,
showered down upon them in thunderstorms
and soft, spring rain;
which calls them even now
to serve the One
who brought them together.

The Grail Cup

The most precious substance within you is your waters. Your waters contain your capacity to respond. This is your capacity to give your heart. It is the nature of your waters, which carry your emotional body, to respond to something. So your heart will be given to someone or something. That is its nature. The only question is to what.

The human world wants your heart. The world wants your response. Advertisers want it. Politicians want it. So do the religions of the world and people who have something they want to sell to you. So do people who are looking for love. They all know that if they get your heart, they will get the rest of you—your thoughts, your labor, your hopes and dreams, and your money.

Sometimes the world captures a person's heart through appealing to narcissism and greed. Sometimes it is through fear—fear about survival, doing the wrong thing, or being irresponsible. No one's heart belongs to the world that way. That kind of heart attachment imprisons people and tears them apart.

Your heart belongs to the sun—to the radiant center of your Being. When your heart turns toward the sun rising in you, it responds easily and naturally. Any time that has happened, you have been lifted up by your feeling response. You have been set free. You have found peace. And then you could let your feelings flow to your world—to people near and far—in a way that brought blessing, in a way that liberated your soul.

The mythic stories of the Holy Grail are about this experience. The Grail is a symbol of the waters of our emotional body, our lifeblood, held within us and offered to the radiant source of our Being. In the story, Parsifal is asked, "Whom does the Grail serve?" He is unable to find the Grail until he offers the true answer to the question, "The Grail serves the Grail King." The sun is the sovereign aspect of a person, symbolized by the Grail King, and our emotional body is at peace when it is surrendered to the sovereign. Our emotional body is the Holy Grail when it is offered to the sun. And when it is, it overflows and is shared with our creative field. As it's said, "My cup runneth over."

Have you had the experience of trying to change something in your creative field, only to find that the shape and pattern of what you were trying to change kept reverting back to how it had been? You might have been trying to change something in yourself or in another person, or in a group of people. It could be an old habit that just won't go away. It could be an old way of thinking about things. It might just be that you, or others, feel continually tired and uninspired.

If you have that experience, think about this: perhaps something has to melt and flow in you or other people. You might be working with water that has turned to solid—to ice. Perhaps there is a way that your grail cup has to be offered up to the sun. Perhaps there is a way you could invite other people to let their hearts melt. Maybe your sun needs to come out for them. Even a little bit of melting could save a lot of hard work—the hard work of trying to make yourself or other people change, because nothing really changes without a melting of the heart.

Perhaps that person who is making your life difficult in your workplace could use the warmth of some kind words from you. Or perhaps someone close to you needs to feel your care.

What is one situation where you intuitively feel that something has to melt in you or someone around you? What is one action that you could take to melt the icy waters?

Cause

Humanity has fallen victim to the idea that the causative factors in the human experience lie in the space-time continuum. It seems easier to believe that the causative factors in our life happen away from us, as opposed to inside us, and in the past or the future as opposed to the present. Here is an example from the scientific world.

The most prevalent theory of Creation in the postmodern world is the Big Bang Theory. Over several decades, there is increasing evidence that points to it as the most likely beginning of the universe. At the same time, there continue to be scientists and others who believe in alternative theories of Creation. Whatever theory might be true, it is hard to miss the fact that the theory of the Big Bang appeals to the human inclination to believe that the cause of human experience is not us—it is outside us, and in the space-time continuum.

Scientists believe that the Big Bang occurred a long, long time ago—about 14 billion years. Can the cause of the human experience become any more remote than that? In some respects, the belief in the Big Bang Theory can have an impact on human experience that is similar to the belief in a God in heaven, remote from the human world and outside of human beings. Both beliefs can be disempowering.

Neither of these beliefs *has* to engender the experience of being a victim of forces outside a person's own making, but they often do. What if the Big Bang didn't just happen far away and a long, long time ago? What if the Big Bang is occurring right now? What if the Big Bang is occurring through you? There is a remarkable explosion of consciousness and energy, and the creation of a world happening through you in this moment.

Where did it come from? You would probably have to say you don't know, except in theory or belief. Scientists don't know where the Big Bang came from either. And if there was a Big Bang, what was there before that? However far back we go, the real origin of the space-time continuum defies mental encompassment.

Perhaps the reality in which you live wasn't just inherited out of the past. Perhaps you are creating it right now. And if you are, how do you like what you are creating? Is there anything you want to create differently?

The cause of creation is entering the space-time continuum from a place of origin that is outside it. The word *eternal* makes reference to something outside of time. The word *infinite* speaks of a reality beyond space. Most people would say that they don't know what the eternal or the infinite are. They know more about what they aren't than what they are. The world of the infinite and the eternal is not the world of space and time. But you are most happy, most fulfilled when you receive the inspiration and energy that comes to you from this hidden world of potential—this quantum reality of what could be.

From the usual scientific standpoint, the cause of things is seen as being in the space-time continuum. One object or physical energy acts on another. The causative factors in creation are understood to be an objective reality operating in the space-time continuum. For instance, Newton discovered the Law of Gravity when he watched the gravity of the Earth make an apple fall. As true as scientific principles might be at a physical level, they tend to treat everything and everyone as material objects. It treats everything as if it were only a *"what,"* and misses *who* is present.

The cause of Creation is not only creating the world around you but creating *your* world through you. The cause of Creation is not just circumventing your consciousness to impact the creative field in which you live. It is attempting to act in and through you, even as you. And if you let that happen fully, who might you find yourself to be?

You are not the victim of your creative field. You are the creator of it.

What is attempting to create through you? How might you be blocking it?

Love in All Its Glory

Love, in all its glory,
reveals itself to the
tranquil mind
and thankful heart.

So draw near to the majesty,
embrace the peace within you,
and so be embraced by love itself,
which is in your every breath.

This is the day
to let go of all old things,
and even if you have been born
many times before,
to enter this world now
as if for the first time.

Darkness

The waters of your Being are the depth of your awareness. At the beginning of the creative process, darkness is on the face of the deep. And because every moment is a beginning, the darkness of your waters is present with you now. Your darkness is the unformed and the unknown. It is the unshaped depth of consciousness that powers your emotions, and it is the unformed potential of life.

How you hold darkness in your life is a critical factor. You can believe it shouldn't be there, that it's something to be dreaded, and something to be covered over and avoided. Or you can learn to welcome it.

The human world has obscured darkness. The use of artificial illumination has chased away the darkness of night. There are many things that obscure the darkness of the deep that's present in all people—television, the Internet, and obsessive work, to name a few. How can there be creativity in your life if you don't make friends with your darkness?

Darkness is a reservoir. When you welcome your own darkness, you embrace a great pool of substance. You embrace the source of your sexual response. And when the focus of your awareness touches that pool, creative vibration moves through you to activate it. We become powerful in our life when we not only welcome the darkness but when we activate the darkness by touching it with our conscious awareness. Only then can something new happen.

All too often, the human experience is utterly too predictable. That's what happens when a person is out of touch with their own darkness and tries to create a life in the image of what is already in form around them—in the image of other people, in the image of their family, friends, or community. Or in the image presented by mass media. You can only live your own original life when it is created out of the dark waters in the depth of your soul.

To accept the darkness in your creative field, you have to accept that you don't know how your life will turn out. You don't know how your world will turn out. You have to accept that you cannot see all that is present in your depth or in the depth of other people. There is unpredictability in the darkness.

As you welcome the darkness in your creative field and let your warmth touch it, you find that the darkness is not just blank. It is a well of unformed possibility, waiting for the activation of consciousness. As you bring your warmth to the darkness of your creative field, new forms of life are conceived in places that you can't see—in the depths of your own soul, in the depths of people you touch, in the depth of the creative field. This is the potential for new creation, new people showing up in your life, and new levels of experience.

At the same time, there might be existing forms, existing structures lying in the deep. Sometimes these forms have life, like a relationship that is creative or a project that is going well. Sometimes there are forms that are old and broken—a relationship that is ready to be over, a way of thinking about yourself that keeps you in a box, or a stale experience that is well past its sell-by date. Or it might be the leftover feeling from a hurtful experience long ago.

When you bring the warmth of the sun to the depth of your creative field, you'll find structures in the dark waters of your soul that are ready to melt. And as they melt, they might break. It might feel like a meltdown. It might feel like a breakdown. Sometimes a whole group of people feel that way. As you bring the warmth of the sun, you bring a melting of the heart. You are letting there be a breakthrough, not just a breakdown. So remind people, the darkness is good. The melting is good. The breakthrough is good. Remind them that they are not the forms in their life that are melting and breaking. They are the warmth of the sun that is doing this good work.

Put in other terms, we are talking about Mother and Father God. The Mother principle is the depth of the substance of the deep. No one knows enlightenment, no one brings light to the world, without welcoming the Mother to their experience. It is the Father principle, the activating vibration working through consciousness, that has union with the Mother, and it is that union that brings light.

Sometimes another person can put us in touch with the warmth of the sun—the Father principle. That is what happened for me as a 17-year-old in the Catskills. I had the honor of assisting the young Japanese man to feel that radiance in Nagano. For me, for anyone, that connection is the beginning of the healing of the heart. But to make the connection, you have to expose the darkness of the Mother within you to the warmth of the sun.

How can you welcome the Mother into your experience? How can you allow the Father to join with the Mother to bring the light into the world?

Generosity

Thought about in a limited way, the word *generosity* might relate to gift-giving, or to tipping the wait staff at a restaurant. The root of the word is from the Latin, *genus*, the same as the root of the word *gene*, and it relates to something we have at birth. So *generosity* is about a person's innate giving capacity, and a person who is generous is one who is in touch with that capacity.

Generosity is a quality that applies to every aspect of life. It can relate to physical things or even to your handling of money, but it is far more than that. It is the experience that you have more to give in any area of your life. More creative thought to give to a problem. More love to give to another person. More stamina and endurance to give to a project you have undertaken.

Physically, you might become tired. Mentally, you might run out of ideas. And emotionally you might feel you have come to the end of your patience and your forgiveness for another person. When you get in touch with your innate generosity, you find your second wind. Your thoughts are out of the box, and you find a way, when it seemed like there was no way. You find that patience and forgiveness doesn't stop based on how someone else behaves. It is part of who you are.

For most people, there are times in their life when they feel they have no more left to give. At a practical level, that is undoubtedly true for anyone at times. But often, the difference between a life of pleasure and fulfillment and one of limitation and frustration is the difference between finding your generosity and losing it.

So how do you change your experience from "running on empty" to your "cup overflowing"? The answer is so profound, so deep, and yet so simple that it tends to escape people. The answer is gratitude for what we are receiving from the universe. It might not be what you think you want and it might not be "how you like it."

But the universe is being generous with you. For starters, it is giving you life right now! And now! And now! It gave you the opportunity to experience your whole life, with all its drama. It gave you people to be with, even though your relationships with them can be difficult sometimes. The more you give thanks for the generosity of the universe, the more your cup is filled. The more you live your life with a thankful heart, the more you have to be thankful for.

Do you like to give gifts to someone who doesn't appreciate them? Of course not!

So if there is an area of your life where it feels like your tank is on empty—an area in which it feels like you've done everything you can do, or where you have been as kind and warm as you can be, or you have tried to think of a good solution to a hard problem and still can't find it—don't shame yourself. Self-shaming doesn't bring generosity. It doesn't bring the more you are looking for.

Be kind to yourself. Thank yourself for all you have done up to now. Be grateful for all the universe has given to you. In your gratitude, can you feel how generosity is still available to you? Drink it up. You have just gotten back in touch with your own generous nature, with all you have to give. If you can receive with gratitude the blessing that life is giving you, you have taken a step to bringing generosity to your creative field.

How can you be warm to yourself?
What can you be grateful to yourself for doing or experiencing?

The radiance of the sun is always generous. The truth is, you are a sun for your creative field, even when you have temporarily lost touch with that reality. And the only way to reconnect with it is to receive and to give the generosity of your own radiance.

The Voice of Being

I am the voice of Being,
Speaking in human hearts and minds.

I am the living Word,
Creative vibration born in the highest heaven.

I am the sacred presence,
Which lives at the heart of all creation.

I have more faces than there are rocks in the desert,
Or stones on the ocean beach.

I have been here many lifetimes
Through all history and before.

I am born again with each baby who comes into the world,
With each inspired thought,
Every longing for home.
And I am present with each one as they leave.

I am the voice of Being,
The sacred presence of the One Who Dwells.

I call all people,
All lands,
All kingdoms,
To my spirit.

I invite all hearts to melt,
All consciousness to turn
To face me and know me as I am.

I am heard by the innocent,
By the open-hearted,
By the one who is not too proud,
Nor too humble to see my face.

I am heard by those who know
That human effort,
Human belief,
Human feeling
Alone is futile.

And that all understanding,
All compassion,
All power,
And life itself
Abide in me.

I am your voice,
And the true voice of every man,
Every woman,
Of all human being.

Hear me,
Know me,
Embrace my spirit,
Your spirit, now.
Be me in human flesh.

I am the voice of Being,
The sacred presence of the Living God.

God the Possible

God is the Possible. Seen this way, we all have a relationship with God, whether we think we believe in God or not. Every human being has a relationship with what they have not yet thought about, what hasn't yet entered their feelings, and what has not yet manifested in the forms of their life.

Different people relate to God the Possible differently. Some people's relationship with what has not yet happened makes them believe that there is nothing truly new that could happen. They generally believe that their experience will just keep going the way it has. There will be no miracles. They have life all figured out, and even though the results might not make them happy, those results are predictable. If you ask such people to entertain the new and different—a thought, a feeling, or the possibility of circumstances that have never been before—they are likely to reject it. We have the opportunity to have a different relationship with the possible.

People usually think of the possible as being in the future. The future is an interesting concept. I am not sure it actually exists in the way we think about it. The usual concept is that there is a linear progression, and things are moving out of the future into the present, to then fade into the past. Or we see ourselves as moving through time from the past, through the present, and on to the future. But it is hard to prove that the future exists. Has anyone visited the future and come back to report on it? Our mind can ponder what it might think of as the future. But we cannot really go there. By the time we experience life, it is in the present.

Maybe the possible is not really in the future. Maybe there are possibilities with us now in a premanifest state. It could be that all of what has not yet happened is waiting in that premanifest state, like the millions of eggs that a woman carries in her ovaries that have not yet created babies. One of those possibilities is born in the present moment.

I cannot prove by observation this way of understanding the possible, because by definition it is not here yet. You cannot see the premanifest. Is this not how God is? I cannot prove the existence of God by observation, because God is the possible, and the unmanifest, even though we can see what is present that we may understand to be a manifestation of God, or a manifestation of what was only a possibility at some time in the past. What we can observe in our own experience is how our life is different, depending on how we relate to the possible.

These words from the Bible speak about our relationship with God the Possible:

Eye hath not seen, nor ear heard, neither have entered into the heart of man, the things which God hath prepared for them that love him.

Stripped of religion, this verse is about what can happen when we are on good terms with the possible. It makes it clear that, to begin with, we have not even thought about what is possible, much less allowed it to manifest. We have not seen it, we have not heard it, and it has not entered our heart or mind.

What is our role in all this? It is to open ourselves to a relationship with the possible in such a way that its warmth *can* be seen and heard and felt with the heart. When we are open in this way, the possible shows up in our feeling perception and in our thoughts, and perhaps in the people and circumstances around us. But for the possible to have meaning to us, it cannot be *just* in the world around us without being in our feeling perception and in our thoughts, because we would not see it on that basis. We would not be able to recognize it. We would not have the joy of what is possible; we would not appreciate the possible if it were only in our world. It has to enter our heart and mind for it to have value to us.

One of the ways I access God the Possible is by writing songs. It is a process of deep listening to a previously unheard sound. It is a process of discovering, more than a process of inventing. It begins as an essence.

The more I listen to that essence with the ear of the heart, the more that essence takes root in me until it becomes a song.

Our human capacity—our thoughts and feelings and our physical capacity—is made to be a dwelling place for the possible. We are supposed to be a home for the possible, so that it might manifest through us into the world. So open your heart to what is possible in your life. Feel the feelings of the possible. Think the thoughts. It takes believing in something that is not yet here, in this world, but could be if you were open to it. Knowing that at some point it will take bold acts of personal courage for what is possible to manifest in your life.

How can you create a home for what's possible in your life
and feel its warmth?

Chapter Two

THE ATMOSPHERE
OF
UNDERSTANDING

The sun always shines above the clouds.

~ PAUL F. DAVIS ~

The Creative Field

You live in the center of a field of consciousness, mostly your own. There also is the consciousness of other people. Then there is a divine consciousness and presence that fills your creative field. Most importantly for you, your presence fills your creative field. It pervades your body, your thoughts, and your feelings. It touches and surrounds the people in your world. It holds the physical world in which you live in your consciousness.

For your creative field, the conscious awareness you bring is like the atmosphere surrounding our planet. It is the space in which creation occurs. The quality of that atmosphere is critical for life to flourish. If the temperature becomes extremely hot or extremely cold, living things die. If the atmosphere becomes thin, it is hard to breathe. If the mix of oxygen, carbon dioxide, and other gases changes, it affects the forms of life. Your conscious awareness is the air that your creative field depends on for life.

Dr. Stephen R. Covey, author of *The Seven Habits of Highly Effective People,* says that listening to another person is like giving them oxygen. By doing so, we have the opportunity to bring a quality of consciousness to other people that assists them to flourish. In fact, we affect others in this way. The people in your world are constantly responding to the way you think about them. That is partly because of specific things you say.

Additionally, social scientists who have studied human communication tell us that much of what we convey to other people is through body language. Facial expressions, posture, and tone of voice can communicate more powerfully than the words we use. They are part of the music of what we communicate to others. And if the words and music don't match, the people in our creative field respond to that confusion.

Beyond words, and beyond body language, there are subtler ways that our consciousness pervades our creative field and affects it profoundly. A prayer spoken for the well-being of another brings them greater possibility of increasing health, even if they live halfway around the world. The field of creative thought held by a group of people around a project increases the likelihood that it will succeed. An energy field of love helps children to thrive.

Your world is living in the field of your conscious awareness. You might have focused on how you communicate what you are thinking to other people. But whatever you are thinking, whatever the quality of your consciousness, your creative field lives within it. Your consciousness provides a home for the people of your world. They can have a place where they feel like they belong because they are in your field.

Most people live their life with the understanding that they are a small part of a big world. While that is true at a physical level, there is another way to look at it. From the standpoint of your mental capacity, your conscious awareness is big enough to hold everything and everyone in your world. They all live there, in your mind, and in the atmosphere created by your thoughts.

If you experience yourself as part of a big world, you will find yourself assessing the people and places in that world to determine which ones you like and which ones you want to avoid. From the perspective of that worldview, what else would you do?

When you know that the world you are experiencing is happening within your own mind as well as around you, the way you play in your life changes. You begin to understand that you can change your experience by surrounding the people and circumstances that live in your consciousness with the atmosphere that comes from your creative thought. You can surround them with a spirit of understanding and positive intention. You can choose to see past people's limitations and faults, and give them a place, in your thoughts, where they can be themselves.

Of course, you could also be harshly critical of the people and circumstances of your life. You could act as judge, jury, and executioner, passing out harsh condemnations in your mind when people don't act the way you believe they should. However, when you understand that the people in your life populate your mind as well as your world, you become more interested in their well-being.

If you see someone as outside of you, it probably seems difficult to hold consistent positive thoughts. From that perspective, it is impossible. When you understand that the people and circumstances of your life are living within your consciousness, your innate ability to surround them with compassion and understanding kicks in.

The closest analogy, physically speaking, is of a mother carrying a child during pregnancy. There is discomfort as the child develops and the mother's body changes over the course of the nine months. What really matters, though, is that the life force within the mother is providing the womb in which a human being can initiate its life and develop. Within that womb is the amniotic fluid surrounding the child, and the fluids within the child itself. Your mind has that kind of capacity for the cycles of creation in your world. Your mind can be a womb in which creation is conceived, and where it develops and grows. Your mind has a part to play in holding the waters of your world so that things can grow.

TRY THIS: *Think of someone in your creative field who is facing a challenge. Bring them closely to mind and say their name to yourself.*

Then speak words that create an atmosphere in which this person is most likely to succeed, perhaps something like this:

Welcome home.

I understand you are facing a challenge.

I forgive you for any limitations you have had in handling this challenge.

I see you for who you are.

I wish you the best.

Words like this might not make sense in terms of external reality. But they can be part of holding a creative atmosphere for a person in your world.

Water and Air

You have probably noticed that there is a connection between how you think and how you feel. If your emotions are the deep waters of your soul, then your thoughts are the atmosphere—the air. In the physical world, atmospheric disturbance roils the waters of the rivers, lakes, and oceans. Wind can create wave heights close to 100 feet on an open ocean.

Just as the air is a force of nature that affects the waters around the globe, your thoughts affect the waters of your soul. Start thinking about the bad things that could happen to you soon. Think about how someone close to you has wronged you in some way. Or picture the last time you did something you really regret. See how it feels to think those thoughts. Are your emotional waters beginning to stir? If you keep it up, your heart rate might change and your bodily fluids could even change significantly.

Now think of someone who is dear to you. Think of something you like to do. Imagine being in a place you love. Your emotional body has probably begun to relax.

Your thoughts and your feelings have a magical relationship that works according to its own rules. Your mind might be able to direct your body to do things and, within limits, your body will obey. Your mind might judge that a certain physical action is right, and another action is wrong. But when your mind tries to tell your feelings what to do, as if they were just another appendage, it doesn't work so well. And judging your negative feelings doesn't usually help either. Giving that kind of direction and judging right from wrong might work when it comes to the physical world. It doesn't work well in matters of the heart.

The simple truth is that the emotional realm responds to a tranquil mind that is willing to understand it. This certainly works among people. Think about the relief it can bring to your heart when you share what you are feeling with someone who really understands you. Even if they don't "side with you" or agree with you. Just being heard, seen, and understood can put the heart at ease. Psychologist Carl Rogers called it empathic listening. But you don't have to be a psychologist to listen deeply to what is in the heart of another person and convey simply this, "I understand."

You can practice sharing your feelings openly with someone who will listen to you without judgment, and you can practice listening to someone else. You can practice understanding other people's feelings, and practice being understood. Like many internal dynamics, it is easier to practice how mind and emotions relate among people than it is to practice how they relate within you.

Nonetheless, the person you have the greatest opportunity to understand is you. Your feelings, your life history, the parts of you that feel hurt, the parts of you that feel vulnerable. Take time to sit down and ask how you are feeling and why. Be willing to listen to what your emotions have to say. If you will promise not to inflict judging, shaming thoughts on yourself, you might be surprised at what you will hear. Be willing to simply say, "I understand."

One of the great teaching stories about Jesus spoke of the way that a tranquil mind can calm the emotional waters. It is the story of the storm on the Sea of Galilee. In the middle of the storm, his disciples wakened him from sleep. He arose and spoke these words, "Peace, be still." The wind ceased, and there was a great calm.

Is there a situation or circumstance around which you are judging and shaming yourself? Contemplate this and then say to yourself,
"I understand. Peace, be still."
How do you feel now?

Your tranquil mind has the power to bring peace and calm to the emotional waters of your creative field—to your own emotions and to the emotional waters of the people in your world.

The Difference Between Breathing and Suffocation

I learned a lot about atmosphere when I moved to New York City. I had studied to be a teacher, earning a four-year degree and then a master's degree in educational administration at the University of California in Riverside. By the time I moved to Woodhaven, Queens, in New York City in 1982, I had taught school in Southern California for two years and had lived in residential spiritual communities for a total of six years. After moving to New York, the teaching job that had been offered to me fell through, so I went to work doing business administration in an office downtown on Water Street. I was 28 years old. This was different.

I had always found that I could feel the atmosphere of Manhattan crossing the George Washington Bridge onto the island. Beyond the smog, the sirens, and the sometimes stale and pungent odor of the city, there is the energy—a constant hum of human hubbub. And as I took the ramp of the bridge onto the West Side Highway, I felt I was entering that hubbub—the epitome of "the world" that is New York . . . the city.

In 1986, I moved into a small one-bedroom apartment with Joyce and our two-year-old daughter, Helena. We treated the living room as a studio apartment, complete with foldout futon mattress. Helena got the bedroom. The apartment was on 14th Street, just off Union Square, facing south on the tenth floor. We could see the Twin Towers out of our picture window.

Fourteenth Street runs east and west across Manhattan, a long island running north and south. Between the East River and the Hudson River, it is an important route for vehicles crossing the island. And, as we found out, a particularly important route for crosstown buses and trucks in the middle of the night.

With a genius and ingenuity reserved for the city of New York, the huge pothole in the street below us was covered with a large metal plate. No one drove into the gaping hole it covered. And during the day, the sound of vehicles driving over it in long lines tended to blend into the sounds of the city. We weren't there to notice it anyway on the weekdays.

Evenings and nighttime were a different story. The plate did not sit evenly on the pavement on the edge of the pothole, so every axle driving over that hulking piece of metal rattled it. *Ker-chunk, ker-chunk . . . ker-chunk, ker-chunk . . .* It went on all night. Letters to the city accomplished nothing. *Ker-chunk, ker-chunk . . . ker-chunk, ker-chunk . . .*

This was my New York experience. I was drowning in the noise and the smell of the city. Car horns, sirens, loud stereos, cigarettes, smog, and the odor of urine. More than that, I was drowning in the cloud of energy that was the city. I couldn't breathe.

We could not afford to own a car, so escape out of the city was difficult. I felt trapped. I obsessed over plans to escape on weekends.

When can I leave this place permanently?

A year after we moved there, I had a conversation with a friend. He told me about a woman he knew who lived in London, England, and the transformation of her own experience of that city. She had listened to the sounds of a subway and had this transforming thought: *Maybe these sounds could energize me.*

The thought took root in my mind. I applied it to the number four subway line I rode nearly every day and to the cars, the buses, and the constant roar of the city. It wasn't long before I began feeling the human energy of all the people I passed on the street as energizing me. Even the metal plate on 14th Street became my friend.

In the middle of this transformation, I had a little talk with myself. *Dave, you might never leave this city. You might be destined to be here for the rest of your life. Get used to it!*

I felt myself rising through the cloud. It was loving me, not assaulting me. It was energizing. I saw myself rising to the top of it as if it were a giant pillow, buoying me up. I could breathe not only the atmosphere of the city, but the clear air above it. I could feel the warmth and light of the sun shining through that air.

New York became my city. I felt connected to all of it. I felt the sun shining through me to all of its people. They became my people, and I became their friend.

The city became our playground. I started walking the 41 blocks to work every morning, downtown from 14th Street to Maiden Lane, through Greenwich Village, Soho, and Little Italy every morning. I relished the grocery stores opening and the espresso shop owners straightening up from the night before. The people fascinated me—on the street, in the subway, in restaurants! We began to meet like-minded people who experienced the city from a similar spiritual perspective.

I was offered a job in Stamford, Connecticut, in 1990, and after a year of reverse commuting from the city, we moved there. The time had come to leave, but not because I lost any affection for New York. Two years later, when Helena was eight years old, I asked her how she liked living in Stamford. Her reply, after some serious thought, was, "I like Stamford okay. But I'm really a city girl at heart."

When the Twin Towers fell on 9/11, it was a tragic loss for my family and me. I felt I had let my city down because I was not there for its time of trial. I wrote a song that expressed my love for all that the city was to me. The song included these words:

Boats in her harbor bring her gifts,
Her outstretched arms our spirits lift,
Her streets paved with steps of gold,
Now her story will be told.

My experience in New York was a great lesson in my life. I either accept the atmosphere around me for what it is and let it energize me, or I become the victim of it. And if I accept it, I attain a mastery by virtue of something that I cannot fully explain.

Acceptance. It's the difference between breathing and suffocation. Accept the world around you. Breathe deep.

Emotional Intelligence

Have you ever noticed how gullible people tend to be? It's rare that a man ever gets a date with a woman because of the car he is driving. But men must be falling for car ads with sexy women, because the car manufacturers keep showing them. There are politicians and news commentators who are plainly arrogant, incompetent, hateful, and biased, but the general populace votes for them and listens to what they have to say in great numbers anyway. And most people have their own stories of ideas they embraced, only to find out later that those ideas were false and led to disaster.

The truth is that the emotional body is ready to listen to the thoughts of somebody, and it is not necessarily wise about who the ideas come from or what they are. It is the nature of the emotional body to respond to ideas. The only question is, which ones? Without the assistance of some clear thinking, the waters of the human soul can embrace ideas that lead to unhappiness and personal destruction; simple ideas, such as "I could never meet a partner who loves me," or "I am a bad person," become believable after enough repetition. Emotions are subject to the power of suggestion, a dynamic made famous by hypnotists and at work daily in people's lives.

Dr. Masaru Emoto's work, published in *Messages from Water and the Universe*, shows that thoughts and words that carry strong intention, either positive or negative, affect the structure of water. If that is true for water that is *outside* the human body, what is the impact your thoughts and words have on the fluids *inside* your body? Or the impact on your emotions?

It can be frightening to think about the impact of the negative thoughts and words your emotions have been exposed to over the course of a lifetime—from you and other people. And the sad fact is that the emotional body of humanity as a whole has already been impacted for millennia by negative, self-shaming, self-accusing thoughts that have lodged in our collective feeling realm. Like old tires at the bottom of a polluted pond, there they sit, dragged to the surface at the most inopportune moments by current events that latch on to them and drag them up. The more you get to know people, the more you understand that people everywhere share this condition.

Knowing how irrational emotions can be, many people, particularly in the Western world, have decided they want an emotional appendectomy—that their emotional realm is a vestigial organ of an irrelevant, earlier part of their life. They have decided that they could be more successful without having to endure their own irrational feelings or the feelings of other people.

So they try to live their life as if feelings don't matter. That can be an effective strategy—until it backfires—and most of the people around you feel totally alienated from you because you are so cold. Then you realize that you are miserable even though you have accumulated financial wealth, and your health fails because you have cut off the medium through which you experience your own vitality—your emotions.

Emotional intelligence begins with the awareness that your feeling nature is the primal aspect of your human experience. You can't get rid of it, nor should you. It is you at your most innocent, your most open, your most vulnerable. It is you, at your neediest, as a baby and as a child and even in utero. Your feelings are your contact with the primal substance of creation—the waters from which your life and your world are born. Those waters connect you more deeply with your own soul, and with the people around you.

Fortunately, the same dynamic between thought and feeling that creates damage in the emotional body can assist you to let your emotions flow, so that your life is empowered by your feelings, not debilitated by them. With your thoughts and with your words, you can create a safe atmosphere where you welcome your emotions. You can be the one that tells your feelings what they need to hear—not someone else, not the TV, not the tapes in your head of your parents, your teachers, and anyone else in your life who might have told you things that were not true to what your life is about, not true to what is in the depth of your soul.

Having emotional intelligence does not mean that how you feel has to determine what you do. (That's where the *intelligence* part comes in.) It simply means that you have learned to appreciate and invite your own emotional flow. You understand that you feel all kinds of wonderful, irrational, horrible, fearful, and crazy things. And that when you create a place where those feelings can be present without being hidden or shamed, they contribute to a fulfilled life. That way, your feelings respond to your creative thought, not the negative thinking of someone else. Anyway, you cannot get rid of your feelings. You might as well find a good way for them to contribute to your life.

Think of it this way: your thoughts and your feelings could be friends. Your thinking could create an atmosphere of safety in which your feelings are at home. Your thoughts could arouse your feelings in inspiring ways. And your feelings could empower your thoughts with passion. Your feelings could be with you as you do what is yours to do in the world. And if you brought emotional intelligence to your own feelings, maybe you could bring it to the feelings of someone else—a spouse, a friend, an employee, a son or daughter, even the emotional body of a group of people. Held in the atmosphere of your creative way of thinking about those people, they might feel at home and at ease because you are there.

When have you become unconscious of your feelings?
What was the benefit of doing this?
What was the cost of doing this?

Between the Birch Trees and Among the Ferns

Come, let us go, my friend, to that place in the forest
where we once together stood,
between the birch trees and among the ferns
with the sun streaking through
the limbs and leaves and the late-summer air.

Come, let us go to that place
with the elephant-skin beech trees around us,
where we gazed into each other's eyes on that day so long ago
and swore the oath of our lives,
forsaking all but this one thing:
that the granite in our hearts
would be turned inside out in the September sun,
that our best ideas for a world to come
would evaporate like the morning dew
on the maidenhair ferns at our feet;
that eye to eye and man to man,
across whatever roads we had each traveled to that place,
in that clearing in the woods,
in that hour, and in all the hours and days to come,
that for eternity our Being,

from the core to each and every finger and toe,
all of who and what we are, and all of what we have
would be given absolutely and totally to the One we could not name,
but whom we loved with a love so all-consuming
we could no longer deny.

Oh, how my soul aches with that love in this hour,
no less unremitting than on that day,
only turned more gold than crimson,
more like the beech tree than the birch,
as I pray for the fullness of this day's harvest.

So I beseech you, my friend, come,
let us go to that place in the forest where we once together
stood between the birch trees and among the ferns
with the sun streaking through the limbs and leaves
and the late-summer air.
Come with me now to that clearing,
and let us feel together the sun on our now graying hair;
and with that blessing, let us finish what we have yet to do together.

The Cloud

There has been a dark cloud hanging over humanity. It might sound ominous to say so, but it is true, nonetheless. Sometimes when we speak about a dark cloud looming, we are talking about the expectation that something bad is going to happen. When there is a dark cloud in human experience—when the atmosphere surrounding a person or a group of people carries negative energy—it doesn't bode well for the future.

The experience of the negative energy is also a current reality. Certainly, the body of humanity is currently living in a negative energy field. In that sense, there is a dark cloud, and that dark cloud of negative energy has been generated over millennia. It has been fed by the words and actions of people, born out of all kinds of unwholesome spirits—the spirits of hate and fear and all that is born from them. The residue of all those words and all those actions, all that expression on that basis, is a dark cloud. It is the negative side of our collective karma.

Most people are in touch with that cloud without even knowing it. They don't realize that this cloud has descended into their emotional body and affected their thinking. So unwittingly, people all over the world tend to express themselves from out of that cloud, having received the energy of it into their experience.

In the process, people often think that someone else in their world, near or far, has made them experience what they are experiencing and made them act the way they are acting. All the while, what they are unconscious of is that they have been reacting to their experience of this dark cloud in human experience. Through that kind of process, people feed the dark cloud, so it becomes larger for them, and to that degree for all of humanity.

There are people around the world who are celebrating the reality of a different kind of cloud; because while humanity has a legacy that has produced the dark cloud, there is also another kind of legacy. There is the legacy of our spiritual ancestors—men and women of true integrity down through the ages, who have refused to live out of the human energy field as it has been.

There have been people in every generation who have said, "No, I'm going to make a different choice in my life. I'm going to generate a cloud that carries the positive, creative energy, which is the most real thing about me." Living out of that cloud brings something glorious in living, something that brings fulfillment.

This cloud, which is an already-existing energy field, is present and available. When someone awakens to its presence and brings that reality into the world, it becomes more palpable. It becomes easier for more people to connect to it. It becomes easier for our lives to be filled with that reality. That cloud connects people to the source of their own life and the source of all things. They are more themselves when they are acting and living out of that cloud. It reveals the qualities the ancients wrote about, now referred to as glory—brilliance, splendor, magnificence, and majesty.

When you become aware of how this works, you begin to notice what is happening for you spiritually. You become aware of the spirit that you are experiencing in living—the spirit of love, compassion, blessing, and goodwill. You become aware of the tone of what's happening in your own experience, and you begin to notice what happens to that tone, depending on what you do. You find that when your thoughts buy into the hurt feelings within your emotional body, you are buying into the dark cloud. There is a part of us that wants to remove that experience, that doesn't want any part of it. And if you are watching what is happening when you are about to believe in what your hurt feelings are telling you, you can see it and say, "No, I'm not buying."

There is the opportunity to tune in to something else that is readily available. We are here to make it all the more available, so that when people come near to us they are feeling our cloud of glory. When they are feeling our cloud, they are also feeling theirs. They are becoming aware of the higher ranges of their own atmosphere that connect to their core.

When people are having that experience together, they experience what is most true at the center of their creative field. They find unity, and the dark clouds that can bring contention and confusion dissipate.

In the natural world, a dark cloud obscures the radiance of the sun. This cloud of glory lets the radiance of who you are be conveyed to the world. People can feel your light through the generation of this cloud; they can feel the warmth that emanates from your sun through this cloud. And they can remember those qualities about themselves. This is a cloud that opens a portal to the invisible radiance at your core and allows it to be glimpsed by others who have eyes to see.

You might say that this is the biggest challenge a human being could have—the work of finding a way to let the unseen and the unheard that is at their core be seen and heard. It is seen and heard through this cloud of light and glory. The creation of this cloud is a building process. And if the dark cloud over humanity has taken millennia to build, this cloud will take some time too.

There are people around the world who have embarked on this journey. The journey brings all kinds of new experience because there is the generation of the cloud of glory through which those experiences occur. No one knows where that journey will go, for themselves personally or for the body of humanity. No one really knows what is possible, even though they might have ideas about it.

But you know what you touch as this cloud of light and glory thickens in your experience. That changes your experience and, as it does, that has powerful and profound implications for the world. It changes the people around you as they begin to touch this cloud of light and glory in you, and therefore touch it in themselves. In that sense, this cloud is contagious and it invites everyone to take responsibility for contributing to the generation of it.

As any group of people care more about contributing to the collective cloud of glory for all of humanity than they care about their own fulfillment as isolated human beings, or as a group, they experience something amazing. They experience this cloud collectively, and it has profound implications for them individually and together.

At first it seems like this is a personal, individual journey, and it has to start that way. But what people find is that the individual journey only goes so far until they see that their future is connected to a much larger destiny that involves all of humanity, and Planet Earth as a whole. They find that their own fate and destiny only make sense in that larger context.

As much as they might try to work out their own life on a purely individual basis, that attempt keeps them locked into the dark cloud, because that kind of attempt is based in self-interest. And in self-interest they are locked into the hurts that have lodged in the emotional body of humanity, and the human state as it has been. They become free as they invest in the collective future of humanity because they are investing in the cloud of glory for all humanity.

It might seem like the way to achieve personal happiness and fulfillment is to focus mostly on what is happening for you personally, and that you have nothing to offer that makes a difference to the world. But that is dark-cloud thinking, because in fact exactly the opposite is true: Life becomes easy and fun and joyful when you see that you are here to contribute to the destiny of humanity.

How are you contributing to the destiny of humankind?
Start with the simplest of things, like how you greet the people in your life.

Creation Math

There is mathematics to all of Creation—mathematical patterns that replicate throughout the universe, from the atom to the stars—and human beings are no exception. In his book *The Tao and Its Characteristics* (Chapter 42) Lao-Tzu alludes to the most basic of mathematical patterns this way:

The Tao produced One; One produced Two; Two produced Three; Three produced All things.

The brilliant design of Creation begins with the One. Out of the One, the whole pattern of your life is formed and the constellation of all life is born. In the creation of sound, melody, harmony, and rhythm are generated out of a fundamental tone. All colors of light are found in white light. Seeing this unfolding pattern of creation helps you to bring the atmosphere of understanding to every circumstance of your life.

Your Being begins in oneness. It begins in pure, unitary awareness. This is the sun nature that is you at your core. But you were not content to be just this one thing. You, as unitary awareness, are activating the deep of your Being, which is the unformed substance of creation. These are the waters of your Being. This process is occurring all the time at every level, from each and every cell to all your organs and glands and beyond. So you are two—pure, unitary awareness and the deep of Being that is activated by that awareness. And still, these two things are aspects of the one reality of you.

All form is created by the dynamic of Two—the activation of the deep of your Being by your sun nature. And there is no dynamic without two. Relationship always requires two. Oneness alone is static.

The Two produces the Three—the embodiment of you in form. Most of the forms of you as a person cannot be seen with the naked eye. Most of what is happening in the creation around you cannot be seen with the naked eye. So most people cannot see the majesty of unfolding

Being. That majesty includes the form of their own Being at all levels. Even most of our physical form is hidden under a layer of skin that is usually mostly covered with clothes. Beyond the physical forms there are thoughts, emotions, and energies that manifest who we are.

These words of Krishna from Chapter 11 of the Bhagavad-Gita tell of this common inability to see the forms of Being. They also tell that the only way to see the totality of Being is with the sight of pure awareness that created it all, represented by Krishna in the text.

Gaze, then, thou Son of Pritha! I manifest for thee
Those hundred thousand thousand shapes that clothe my Mystery:
I show thee all my semblances, infinite, rich, divine,
My changeful hues, my countless forms. See! in this face of mine . . . see
Wonders unnumbered, Indian Prince! revealed to none save thee.
Behold! this is the Universe! — Look! what is live and dead
I gather all in one—in Me! Gaze, as thy lips have said,
On GOD ETERNAL, VERY GOD! See ME! what thou prayest!
Thou canst not!—nor, with human eyes, Arjuna! ever mayest!
Therefore I give thee sense divine. Have other eyes, new light!
And, look! This is My glory, unveiled to mortal sight!

Becoming a sun, you are gaining sight as a human being so that you can see the majesty of creation. You are bringing understanding to your human experience.

Four Aspects of Humanity

Ancient Briton Sun Cross

This ancient Briton sun cross symbolizes four cosmic forces at work in the human experience. The elemental names for those forces are water, air, earth, and fire. If you were a Creator Being with four cosmic forces, and you were ready to incarnate in living flesh, wouldn't you create a form that was uniquely suited to manifest those four cosmic forces? That is exactly what happened. Your emotional, mental, physical, and spiritual bodies are instruments for your incarnation and your creative power.

Cosmic Force	Human Capacity
Water	Emotional Body
Air	Mental Body
Earth	Physical Body
Fire	Spiritual Body

The four forces that work through all of Creation never work solo. Each force is always in dynamic relationship with the other three forces. This is true in the human experience. However, for human beings, that creative dynamism is designed to work through the conscious function of the person, or people, involved. That means that you will have to learn to see what is happening in your human capacities if you are going to live a creative life. And you will have to see these four forces at work in your creative field if you want to be able to assist others to come into their own place of mastery.

When the four forces of your Being are flowing freely through you in a balanced way, there is, what the ancient Greeks called, *dunamis*—the ability to create. This ancient word has found its way into modern parlance through such words as *dynamic* and *dynamite*. Ultimately, *dunamis* is the ability to create a world that reflects the wonder and the glory of you, the one who is, in truth, creating it.

To study these four forces in your own experience, you can begin by observing them one by one, noticing how they are manifesting in you. This is a personal practice of self-awareness. It takes shameless honesty and curiosity.

Practice asking yourself these simple questions:
Water / The Emotional Body

What am I feeling?
Air / The Mental Body

What am I believing?
Earth / The Physical Body

What am I doing?
Fire / The Spiritual Body

What am I giving?

When you see and understand these forces at work in your own life, you can begin to see them at work in other people. And then you can see them at work in your creative field. You can gain an understanding of what it takes to bring balance to the working of these forces; for you as a person and for your creative field.

These four forces each bring a foundational aspect of human experience. Water brings flow. Air brings intelligence. Earth brings strength. And Fire brings generosity.

Cosmic Force	Human Capacity	Experience
Water	Emotional Body	Flow
Air	Mental Body	Intelligence
Earth	Physical Body	Strength
Fire	Spiritual Body	Generosity

This is at work in your most immediate creative field—your own humanity. By seeing and naming this pattern, you are bringing the atmosphere of understanding to your human experience.

The Emotional Body

The emotional body is born out of the innocent, primal flow that is natural to infants and which stays with people throughout their life at some level. This is the deep of the waters of your being.

Infants don't have to work to be in that flow. For them, it doesn't have to be practiced or studied. It is just how they are. This flow is the primal energy for a person, in the sense that it is the first energy experienced and it is the root energy behind all the rest of a person's experience. It is a fundamental response to the life within people and to their world.

As people mature, this primal, emotional flow is the juice that energizes and sustains everything else in them. It is the energetic current that is behind all their thinking, doing, and feeling. There are many things a person can do that dampen this primal flow. How a person thinks, acts, and feels can tend to short circuit or suppress the primal flow. But it is not something that has to be built or added to or improved. This foundational aspect of human experience is increased by openness, not by effort. This openness is first experienced with parents.

The emotional body is that part of people that connects easily with what is around them—with the flow of the natural world, with other people, and even with the invisible life energy that courses through the human body. From the standpoint of this aspect of experience, there is no sense of separation from everything else; and therefore, from the standpoint of our own primal flow, there is no need for effort to connect—that is just how things are. The other aspects of our human makeup can modify or inhibit a person's sense of connectedness. But from the standpoint of the emotional body, connection is the reality.

In relationships, people's primal emotional flow is their openness to others and their capacity to receive what another person offers. It is a person's love response in deeply intimate relationships, and the energetic current that is offered to friends, clients, colleagues, or employees.

If the quality of emotional flow is low in a person's life, it might help to explore what has cut off that flow. Or they may simply want to explore good opportunities to open themselves deeply to something or someone who is worthy of their openness.

When people are living from their emotional body, their time orientation tends to be toward the past. They feel more connected with people and places by remembering the past. This might involve nostalgia or longing tied to memory. When people are living in their emotional body, and expressing themselves from there, they typically find it natural to rely on other people and to yield to their influence.

You might also notice that people who are deeply in touch with their emotional body seem like they are melting. They radiate an inner warmth. They might be prone to tears. And it seems like they might go to mush inside at any moment. In the extreme, they might have an emotional meltdown or flare-up. It might seem to others that someone living from the emotional body is trying to be too close and too connected to other people.

In terms of the four archetypes described by Robert Moore and Douglas Gillette in their groundbreaking book on male psychology, *King, Warrior, Magician, Lover: Rediscovering the Archetypes of the Mature Masculine*, this is the archetype of the Lover, which they present in these terms:

> *Along with sensitivity to all inner and outer things comes passion. The Lover's connectedness is not primarily intellectual. It is through feeling. The primal hungers are felt passionately in all of us, at least beneath the surface. But the Lover knows this with a deep knowing. Being close to the unconscious means being close to the "fire"—to the fires of life and, on the biological level, to the fires of the life-engendering metabolic processes. Love, as we all know, is "hot," often "too hot to handle" (page 122).*

Seeing, honoring, and acknowledging your emotional body assists your feelings to find their rightful place in your personal universe. Your emotions become creative in the atmosphere of understanding.

What experiences have you had that assist you to connect with the Lover within you in a positive way? How could you have more of those experiences?

The Mental Body

The mental body brings the cosmic force of air into the human experience. It is the seat of intelligence. Intelligence has most often been equated with the intellectual and academic levels of understanding. More recently, the understanding of human intelligence has expanded to include a wide range of perception and ability. In 1920, American psychologist E. L. Thorndike used the term *social intelligence.*

A theory of multiple intelligences was proposed by American developmental psychologist Howard Gardner in 1983. He named eight types of intelligence: linguistic, logical-mathematical, spatial, bodily-kinesthetic, musical, interpersonal, intrapersonal, and natural. In Dr. Daniel Goleman's best seller *Emotional Intelligence: Why It Can Matter More Than IQ*, he popularized an understanding of intelligence for leaders that, as the title of the book indicates, went well beyond the traditional approach to the topic of intelligence. There is ongoing study as to whether there is a type of intelligence that relates to existential or spiritual matters.

The intelligence of the mental body is a resource that allows people to see the pattern of the world in which they live. It is the understanding of how all the distinct elements of the world relate to one another and the capacity to function in that context. This understanding of patterns extends to the entire human capacity as the intelligence of the mental body brings intelligence to the physical, the emotional, and the spiritual bodies.

People's understanding of the world around them develops when they want to experience something beyond their own primal emotional flow. It is often born out of a curious exploration of the world and the reflection on the underlying patterns that shape it. Or the pursuit of intelligence might be motivated by experiences that are dissatisfying or unfulfilling to a person. Those experiences might cause people to reflect on why events are occurring as they are and on how they, themselves, could be acting in another way to create a different outcome.

This kind of reflection invokes the ability to step back from the immediate pressure of circumstance to contemplate a wider perspective, to perhaps ask questions.

- What happened in the past that led up to this event?
- What are the future implications of the actions I might take now?
- What would this circumstance look like if I were looking at it from a different perspective?
- What would it look like through another person's eyes?

This is the amazing ability of the mind . . . the ability to bring an atmosphere of understanding in which all of a person's humanity can find its place. And as you have this kind of understanding for your own human experience, it becomes easy to extend it to others. You see what is happening for them and why, especially when your atmosphere of understanding is warmed and illuminated by the sun that you are.

The time orientation of the mental body is not locked in past, present, or future. It is the nature of mental function to roam through time—to reflect on the past and to anticipate the future, as well as to observe present circumstances in a detached way.

You might perceive someone who is living from their mental body as cold and calculating. Their time orientation and their ability to reflect on events might give you the perception that they are not fully present. They might be aware of the risks involved in a situation, and that can produce anxiety.

The mental body correlates with the Magician archetype described by Moore and Gillette:

The energies of the Magician archetype, wherever and whenever we encounter them, are twofold. The Magician is the knower and he is the master of technology (page 98).

78

The Magician, then, is the archetype of thoughtfulness and reflection. And, because of that, it is also the energy of introversion. What we mean by introversion is not shyness or timidity but rather the capacity to detach from the inner and outer storms and to connect with deep inner truths and resources (page 108).

In *The Power of Now: A Guide to Spiritual Enlightenment,* spiritual teacher Eckhart Tolle discusses the nature of the human experience from the perspective of the mind:

There is a place for mind and mind knowledge . . . However, when it takes over all aspects of your life, including your relationships with other human beings and with nature, it becomes a monstrous parasite that, unchecked, may well end up killing all life on the planet and finally itself by killing its host (page 45).

Addressing the tendency of the mind to obsess over past and future, Tolle says this:

So break the old pattern of present-moment denial and present-moment resistance. Make it your practice to withdraw attention from past and future whenever possible in everyday life (page 45).

The development of the mental body begins with the baby's exploration of its immediate home world, and it continues through the most profound reflections on the meaning and purpose of life. When brought to any aspect of human function, its intelligence can be a great gift. The mind plays a key role in orchestrating the dynamic of all four forces in human experience.

How easy do you find it to invoke the Magician within you? To see what is happening for you in a cool, detached, reflective kind of way when you need to?

Or do you tend to live your whole life as one of reflection?

The Physical Body

The physical body brings vitality, beauty, and strength through the body and into the person's world. It brings the earth force into play. At a physical level, the exercise of strength is vital to creation. It allows work to be done now, and it brings strength over time, the endurance that allows creations to come to completion.

Seeing and understanding the place that strength has in your life brings appreciation for it. In the atmosphere of your understanding, your strength can find a balanced place in your life.

People's strength protects what is precious to them. It allows them to set boundaries and protect themselves and others physically. Strength is also required to face issues that confront a person, and it is needed to bring the creative process to completion.

As children mature, they find out that there are experiences that they desire in their life that they won't have without effort. They have to work to crawl and then to walk. They have to use their strength to play physically. The child finds out that there are experiences that they can't have just through the emotional body. There is so much that they receive from parents just by being open to it and then crying if they don't get it. But to climb a hill, to play tag, to be involved in a game, they will need to exert their strength and endurance. And the child's strength is being called on if the class bully is shoving them in the hall at school.

Later in life, there are things that people want to happen that will clearly take effort of whatever kind—the work they apply to their career, the effort they make to be of service to others, or the energy of building a family.

Strength is the application of a person's life energy to meet the immediate circumstances they face. This might be to build something or to expand what has already been built. A person might use their strength to fulfill a mission that is important to them or to carry out the wishes of another person. A person's strength might also be used to protect the tender things of the heart.

The time orientation of the physical body is the present. It has to do with addressing what is happening now. You might notice that people who are living from their physical body are accustomed to using their strength in situations with other people. You might perceive them as confrontational and pushy. You might also observe that they have a keen awareness of their own boundaries and when those boundaries are being crossed.

Moore and Gillette describe the Warrior archetype in men, which is a manifestation of the strength which is born out of the physical body.

The Warrior energy, then, no matter what else it may be, is indeed universally present in us men and in the civilizations we create, defend, and extend. It is a vital ingredient in our world-building and plays an important role in extending the benefits of the highest human virtues and cultural achievements to all of humanity (page 79).

While the strength of the physical body often shows up in traditionally male activities, such as extending the boundaries of influence into new places, strength can also show itself in the protection of what has already been created. So the use of strength, or assertiveness, might be for the protection of home and family, which are traditionally associated with the female role. Similar instincts might be brought to larger groups, like the instinct to protect a business enterprise or even a nation.

As the strength of the physical body relates dynamically to the mental body, the emotional body, and the spiritual body, it brings that quality of strength to the function of the other bodies and plays a vital role in letting people live and act in their world.

Can you rely on the strength within you when you need to?
Or do you tend to use excessive strength even when it isn't called for?

The Spiritual Body

The spiritual body is the place in which people entertain what is possible in their life. It is the capacity to believe that something wonderful and creative could occur. As the spiritual body in a person is activated, that faith in what could occur in a person's life leads to a sense of abundance and generosity. It brings the Fire force into play.

As the word is usually used, *generosity* relates to an act in which one person gives liberally to another. The root of the word is similar to the word *genes*, and originally generosity related to being born in a place of high social standing with a calling to give to others. In the broadest possible meaning of the word, it is a name for that quality of human experience that is characterized by the sense that there is more available—more love, more energy, more ideas, more options, and more to offer to others.

People's capacity to love in a generous way is born from their spiritual body. It might be a love of the world in which a person lives and the people in it. It can include the love of family, community, or an organization. From some it might be a love for the whole world. It is also the capacity to love one other person, or even oneself, in a generous, compassionate way.

When you understand that you have a neverending source of the universal power of love within you, then, in the atmosphere of that understanding, your mind, your body, and your emotions learn to make that connection.

The time orientation from the perspective of the spiritual body is the future. The spiritual body is that aspect of people that allows them to believe that things are possible in the future which don't yet exist in form. For people who are living from their spiritual body, the possibilities they sense might be even more real to them than the facts in front of them.

You might notice that people who are living from their spiritual body are quick to celebrate the positive qualities of life. At times, you might perceive this as being boastful or egotistical when people celebrate themselves or others associated closely with them. These people might also appear to be unreasonably hopeful or optimistic. You might observe them encompassing other people and offering kind leadership, and sometimes the way they relate to other people might appear to be condescending.

Moore and Gillette wrote about the King archetype in men. The gender-neutral term for king is the sovereign, which is the archetype associated with the spiritual body.

The mortal man who incarnates the King energy or bears it for a while in the service of his fellow human beings, in the service of the realm (of whatever dimensions), in the service of the cosmos, is almost an interchangeable part, a human vehicle for bringing this ordering and generative archetype into the world and into the lives of human beings (page 50).

In conjunction with his ordering function, the second vital good that the King energy manifests is fertility and blessing (page 58).

The generosity that extends from a healthy spiritual body is a key factor in energizing and empowering the physical, mental, and emotional bodies.

Is it easy or is it difficult for you to be the sovereign in your world?

Four Forces, Six Dynamics, Twelve Experiences

For so many people, what is happening within their own humanity is a mystery. They focus so much on what is happening *to* them that they hardly notice what is happening *within* them. What other people say and do looms large. The events of life tend to fill their conscious space. And only when problems arise in their human capacity do they notice what is happening within them. It could be a physical ailment. Or an emotional flareup, like an angry reaction to someone at work. Or it could be a mental state, like anxiety that demands attention. And for most people, when they are paying attention to something within their human capacity, they are only seeing "what went wrong." They are not seeing the wonder of how they are made inside and how all the aspects of who they are work together.

Think of how your life might change if you brought an atmosphere of understanding to your whole human experience—if you saw the wonder and the beauty of how you are made. And then if, in that understanding, you had a basis for seeing, with compassion, what was out of balance for you. That is what happens when the sun rises in you—when the warmth and light of the sun illuminate your atmosphere and create understanding.

So here is a way to understand how we are all created as human beings—how all the parts of who we are relate to one another dynamically to create an amazing, living whole.

The number of one-to-one relationships between any four things is six. Here are the six relationships possible between the four aspects of your nature.

Spiritual / Emotional

Mental / Emotional

Mental / Physical

Spiritual / Physical

Spiritual / Mental

Emotional / Physical

Does it sound strange to think that different parts of you are in relationship? It is happening all the time at a physical level. The stomach talks to the brain and the adrenal glands send messages to the rest of the body through the bloodstream. Sit down and have a talk with your physical body one day. See what it tells you. Or have a conversation with your emotional body. Open up to the spiritual within you, to the source of your generosity. You might be surprised to hear what it is telling you.

It is difficult to see and understand the dynamic of unseen aspects of your own humanity. Fortunately, our life unfolds in such a way that these dynamics are demonstrated to us among the people in our life from birth. As you begin to understand the nature of the pattern, you see it all around you. There is the mother bringing her generosity to what is flowing in the experience of the baby. There is a person offering intelligent insight to the emotional experience of another. And there is a strong person in service to the spiritual virtues embodied by a respected leader.

These are all examples of the four cosmic forces being embodied by individual human beings. Those individuals are embodying the corresponding human capacity that becomes an instrument for those four cosmic forces.

These forces are also working through groups of people, large and small. In a corporation, the planning department brings intelligence to the physical manifestation of the corporation. The human resource department shows generosity when it demonstrates care for the emotional needs of employees, and the corporation suffers if it fails to do so.

Elemental aspects of human experience are holographic. This means that they reoccur at every level of experience. They are present in the individual, in any group, and as a whole. At every level, the elemental aspects of human experience are designed to comprise a whole entity, a hologram of humanity as a whole and, beyond that, a hologram of the cosmic whole.

The holographic nature of human experience makes it possible to bridge the understanding between individual and group levels of this experience. The dynamics among groups of people can teach a person about the individual experience. And individual experience can teach us something about group dynamics.

The process of human development is the building of these six dynamics so that you, as a Creator Being, have an effective human capacity through which your four cosmic forces can work in dynamic relationship. For humanity as a whole, this is our journey—a path of learning what it means to be in dynamic relationship with one another and to become a whole, unified body of humankind.

The diagram below is a contemporary cross showing the Four Forces in dynamic relationship through the human experience. Aligned with each force is the aspect of the human capacity through which it appears, the aspect of human character associated with that force, and the basic time orientation of people when they see their world from that perspective.

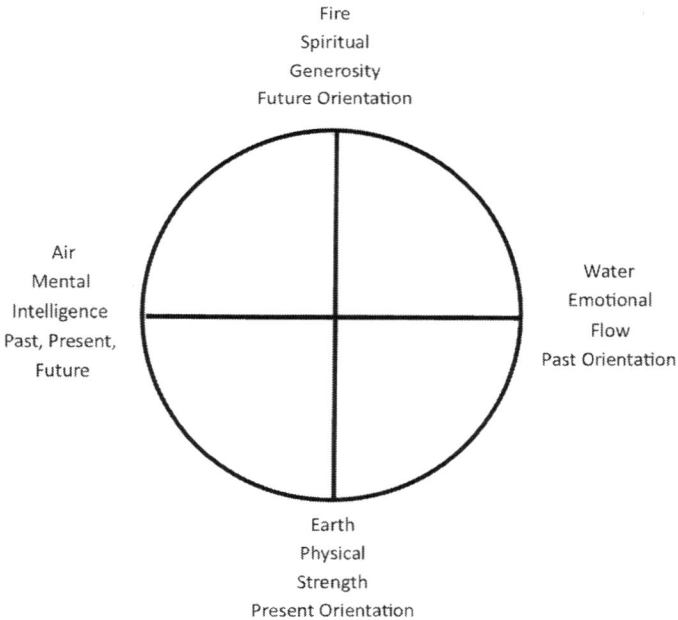

Fire
Spiritual
Generosity
Future Orientation

Air
Mental
Intelligence
Past, Present,
Future

Water
Emotional
Flow
Past Orientation

Earth
Physical
Strength
Present Orientation

You can count six lines in the diagram depicting the six relationships between the Four Forces. The experience of any relationship is unique to the entity who is experiencing it. So each relationship has within it two unique experiences. Altogether, there are four forces through four aspects of your humanity, creating six dynamic relationships, and twelve unique experiences.

For instance, when you are experiencing yourself and your world primarily from the perspective of your mental body, and you think about what you are feeling in your emotional body, you have activated one of the six relationships. You have the experience of relating to your emotions from a mental standpoint.

Others might activate the same relationship while being primarily centered in their emotional body. They are living in the feelings of their emotional body and referencing the thinking of their mental body to gain some intelligence—some insight and perspective—about their emotional experience.

Each of the twelve experiences works in this way. The experience is unique according to which aspect of the human capacity is the primary factor in the person's experience, and which other aspect of the human capacity is in the dynamic. Of course, all four aspects of a person's humanity are in play to some degree all the time. But they don't all fire together in a random, chaotic way.

There is a natural pattern and rhythm to how these twelve experiences appear in a person or in a group and in how they change over time. This is what creates dynamism in the human experience. This pattern is the creative process at work. Understanding of it leads to mastery in your own experience of the creative process.

The first six chapters of this book are each devoted to one of these six dynamics. This chapter you are now reading is called "Understanding," because it reflects the dynamic created when the intelligence of the mental body and the flow of the emotional body are in relationship.

Are you finding it easy to observe what is occurring in your own emotional body without self-judgment? Or if you fall into self-judgment, can you not judge yourself for that?

Reciprocity

The Merriam-Webster dictionary says that to reciprocate is "to give and take mutually; to return in kind or degree; to move forward and backward alternately." The origin of the word *reciprocate* is from the Latin *recipricus*, "returning the same way; alternating."

Reciprocity is an essential aspect of the creative dynamic among people. Let's say you invite someone over for dinner. What would it mean for them to reciprocate? The most obvious way would be for them to say, "Yes, I'll come."

But let's say this relationship has been going on for a while, and you've invited this person over to dinner for a year. Every month you say, "Would you like to come over for dinner?" and the person says, "Sure, I'd love to come!" What are you thinking after a year is over? "Hey, wait a minute—this isn't reciprocity."

Real reciprocity includes mutuality. If one person is always doing the inviting and the hosting, and the other person is just accepting the invitation and enjoying being hosted, there is a lack of mutuality, which requires that both people host and both people are hosted—not all at the same time, but over time.

Mutuality is achieved in relationship because the people in the relationship find a way to alternate in the roles they play. If it doesn't go there in a relationship, and it never goes there, you might sense that something is stuck. It might feel uncomfortable and imbalanced. If you have been inviting that person to dinner every month for a year, you might wonder, "Why don't they invite me for once?" Something breaks down in relationships if they do not move in the direction of reciprocity.

Sometimes reciprocity between two people is fulfilled outside the relationship itself. Think about the relationship between a mother and a daughter. At first, as a baby, the daughter responds to her mother's nurturing by melting in Mother's arms and receiving the love that is given. As a little girl, the daughter might practice reciprocation by caring for her doll. Ultimately, the daughter reciprocates by "paying it forward"—she takes the role of mother for her own child.

Sometimes the opportunity for reciprocity among parents and children is built into the culture of a people. Several years ago, I worked with a young man in Bangkok, Thailand. As is common for young men in Thailand, he spent a year of his life as a monk.

People in that part of the world are conscious of those to whom they owe deference and respect. As this young man told me, when he became a monk, all the deference and respect that he had shown his parents was then shown to him. His culture initiated him into the experience of full reciprocity—he became the elder for that year. And when the year was over, the place of respect was handed back to his parents. He was profoundly changed by the experience.

If a parent does not deliberately create opportunities for reciprocity, it might have to happen without the parent's conscious consent. Isn't that what childhood rebellion is all about? If children aren't finding the opportunity to move into adulthood in a way that is sanctioned by parents, they take matters into their own hands by rebelling.

If reciprocity is not sanctioned in an organizational setting, leaders are put on a pedestal and then knocked down by others. The process might begin with adulation. If the responsibility of leadership is not shared, the time inevitably comes when resentment rises and leaders are undermined.

The dynamic of reciprocity initiates you into the twelve experiences that are created by the Four Forces working through the four aspects of your humanity. If you find something stuck in your own experience or in the experience of other people, there might be a breakdown of reciprocity. Perhaps people were never loved in such a way that they learned to love back. They were never understood in such a way that they learned to understand another person. Or they were never offered the kind of leadership that taught them to come into their own leadership.

Reciprocity is the process by which people are initiated into their own wholeness. When your atmosphere of understanding surrounds the process, you can be the kind of person who heals the places where reciprocity is broken in your own life. You can be a person who invites others into your own full experience of reciprocity.

Are there areas of your life in which it is time for you to come into your own elderhood, or your own mastery?

From Mountain Peaks

The eagle shrieks
From mountain peaks,
And calls to the world below,
To sunlit hills
And a meadow, still.
He invites the world to know
This majestic hour,
This inner power
Which springs from the heart of love,
A world being born,
On this golden morn
Straight from the heavens above.

Over gray streets
And building peaks
He soars above the noise,
Over you
And over me,
We hear his wakening voice.
"Look up!" he cries,
From the brightening sky,

"This is the day foretold,

When heaven's light

Breaks forth on earth,

And a shattered world is made whole."

Chapter Three

THE BURSTS

OF

ACTION

I hope you will go out and let stories, that is life, happen to you,
and that you will work with these stories . . . water them with
your blood and tears and your laughter till they bloom,
till you yourself burst into bloom.

~ CLARISSA PINKOLA ESTÉS ~

A Great Threshold

You cross one of the greatest thresholds in your life when you burst
from intention and idea to action. Everything changes. All the deep
emotions you have for the possibility you have felt deep within your
soul can seem like they are being dashed against the rocks of the real
world. The lofty ideas you have had about the way life should work are
challenged. And you run the risk, as if for the first time, that you will
fail—that what you are attempting will not succeed, that your ideas are
not true or valid in this world, and that your deep feelings will seem
irrelevant to other people.

In taking action, there is a risk of apparent failure. Half the marriages in the United States end in divorce. More than half of small businesses in the United States fail within the first eighteen months. Any time there is an attempt to accomplish something, there is the risk that it will not succeed—at least not the way you expect it to.

In taking action, you are letting all that you have generated in the creative process to this point precipitate a physical act. You are applying your strength to manifest in physical form what you have felt and thought internally. You are taking the intelligence generated through the mental body and letting it direct your physical body.

I have seen people become paralyzed when facing this step in their own life. For some, they would rather retreat to an inner reality of thought and emotion and avoid or downplay the need to act. I have seen groups of people break apart because they would rather think, talk, and feel than do something.

In taking action, Air meets Earth. Intelligence guides strength. For many people, it is a terrifying step, so they seek to avoid action or to act small. For all of us, we are passing a significant threshold in the creative process when we embody what is within us in an action that is visible in the world.

Four Empowering Considerations

Risk

When you face the opportunity to take action, you are also facing all the times in your past when you took an action like the one you are facing now and it did not go well. You are facing all the times that similar attempts in the past left you feeling smaller and weaker and with less faith in yourself than when you began. Someplace, perhaps buried deep inside, you are weighing the risk that you could have that kind of experience again.

Most people shame themselves when they avoid taking action. When action is clearly needed, they might try to shame themselves into the action—especially men, who are told they should be strong and brave.

You can have more understanding than that. You can appreciate the fact that you are wise enough not to subject yourself to the pain of failure when the odds of success are not good. You can assess the risks and rewards of action, and make wise decisions based on your assessment. You can balance the risks of action with the risks of nonaction and choose the better course. You can choose to mitigate the risks in the actions you take. You can embrace the fact that in life, one way or another, you have to act to truly live.

What situation is calling you to burst into action? What are the rewards?
What are the risks? Are there ways that you can mitigate the risks?
Are you being called to act despite the risks?

Self Love

Many people grow up in an environment in which they are rewarded with love if, and only if, they behave in the way that elders want them to behave. They may go on to choose partners in life who treat them the same way. So they get used to living a life full of conditional love. And love that is conditional isn't worth the name.

If you are used to conditional love in your life, then when you are facing the need to act, you might have this horrible problem to face: If you act, you might fail in the eyes of another person, and, if that is so, they might not love you. Worse yet, you might fail in your own eyes and you might not love yourself.

Can you promise to keep loving yourself no matter what the outcome of your actions? Can you walk a path of self-compassion and self-love, whatever the outcome of what you do? The way you act in your world will change if that is so. You will be free to be wise and strong in what you do and in the risks you take.

Embrace the blessing that comes to you in your life, no matter what the outcome of your efforts. Your strength to act will grow.

TRY THIS:

Think of a situation in your life that needs your action.
Think about what might be holding you back from action.
Think about what could go wrong if you do act.
Now say this to yourself,

"Whatever happens. Whatever I choose to do or not do.
Whatever other people think. I am with you. I am for you. I
am supporting you no matter what.
I love you, _____ (use your own name)."

The Best Plan

The plan matters. You might be full of love. You might have performed a good analysis of the risks involved and decided to move forward. You might be full of the courage and strength to act. But if you have a bad plan, your action will not succeed. It will not help you accomplish what you seek to accomplish.

So take time to plan your actions thoughtfully and consciously before you burst into action. It might be a methodically prepared plan created over a long period of time, like the blueprint to a building or the writing of a symphony. It might be a plan that seems to emerge spontaneously only a fraction of a second before the action, like making a pass in a basketball game, like playing piano in an improvisational jazz trio, or like carrying on a creative conversation. Whatever the action, let your intelligence create the pattern for your action. The plan matters.

Facing What Seems Like Failure

Are you prepared to face what seems like failure? Are you prepared to accept it simply as what happened and to let it be the starting point for whatever is next? Are you prepared to let what seems like failure be a learning experience? An opportunity to test your plan?

Here is a short list of highly creative people who experienced large apparent failures before great success. In each case, the apparent failures became unimportant. They became learning experiences that led to large accomplishments.

Henry Ford had five business failures that left him broke before inventing the Model T.

Oprah Winfrey was fired from her job as a reporter and told she was unfit for television.

Winston Churchill failed in every election for public office until he was elected prime minster at age 62 and led England through the Battle of Britain.

Albert Einstein did not speak until he was four and did not read until he was seven and he was expelled from school. His application to the Zurich Polytechnic Institute was rejected.

Isaac Newton did poorly in school and failed at running his family's farm before discovering gravity.

Walt Disney was fired by a newspaper editor because "he lacked imagination and had no good ideas." He had several businesses that ended in bankruptcy.

Nobody likes to fail. You are probably not an exception. But what if you could face your own failure, with all the feelings that go with it? What if you knew that any failure does not define you? Do you think you might be more ready to burst into action?

Through Foundering Seas

I sail my boat
through the foundering seas
past Plum Island
and before the safe harbor
that lies to the east.
It is the kind of drunken chop
that my mother sailed through
years before
when the wind turned
against the Gulf Stream,
and my father lay out cold,
racked with an unknown pain
beneath the deck;
when she sang
against the terrible night
to bring her boat safely
to the Florida shore.

But this is a different storm
on a different day,
and I have not been

at the helm
through such a swallowing sea
with an open craft,
taking on water like this
over the sides.

And never before,
in such a sea
where there is no comforting
roll of the waves that come,
one following another,
but only rising gray swells
that peak at will around us
with the wicked west wind
whipping off their tops
to throw them in our face.
Never before have I carried
my dear only daughter
into such a storm;
her, smiling beside me
as she licks the salt spray off her lips,
unaware of the gray behemoth
lurking in the deep,
ready to swallow us
into its great belly.

O, if I had not departed
from the now distant shore
on this fateful day!
But I set sail
on a golden morn,
and I made a pact
with the sun as he rose
to greet what the sea would bring us.

So I will sing
my mother's song of hope,
and through those tones
will the wind
to carry this vessel,
this child,
this day,
to safety.

Through the Storm

In the summer of 2010, I had the opportunity to go for a two-week sailing trip. We sailed from Point Judith, Rhode Island, into Long Island Sound; out through the East River and past the Statue of Liberty in New York Harbor; and then down the New Jersey coast into Delaware Bay. It was a glorious trip. We even saw dolphins off the coast of New Jersey!

The whole voyage was a learning experience, but the critical point was a storm we encountered. It was Wednesday, June 23, off the coast of Bridgeport, Connecticut.

We were several miles offshore with our daughter, Helena, who was almost 26 years old at the time. For the most part it was a clear and wonderful day, a beautiful day. We watched the dark gray thunderhead cross Long Island Sound and approach Connecticut. We thought we were smart enough to know what direction this menacing-looking storm was moving, and we thought it would pass us by. In fact, we had just put on additional sail, and we were kicking back and relaxing when the storm hit us.

I heard a weather person describe it later as a microburst, in which the wind begins by moving vertically instead of horizontally. When it hits the ground or the water, it spreads out in all directions.

I've sailed for a good part of my life, and I've seen some bad weather. I've been in some large storms in some small boats, but I've *never* seen something like this! The wind whistled through the metal stays holding our mast, ripped off part of our wind indicator and tore up one of our sails. It was hailing, and I don't know just how hard the winds were blowing, but they were blowing hard. We let out our sails, but even with our sails most of the way out, we were heeling. We were broadside to the wind, which is not how you want to be in a storm like that—you want to be either headed up into the wind or away from it, and into the waves or away from them. We had one wave come over the side and into the cockpit.

Helena turned to me and asked, "So what are we going to do?"

In all honesty I said, "I don't know."

She suggested we turn on the engine, which helped us head the boat up into the wind and into the waves.

My crew and I were sorely tested. If you've been in experiences like that, where you know there are lives at risk, you hit a different kind of reality, a no-nonsense reality. When the storm hit, I exhorted my crew to let out the lines on the sails. I said, "Let out the sheet," and when I saw that our boat was still heeling on its side, I raised my voice and I spoke above the storm, "*Let out the sheet!*" There were things that had to happen to preserve the lives of my crew and me and my boat. They had to be the right things and they had to be done—not partway done, but all the way done.

So those are no-nonsense moments when, if people are rising to the occasion, they are letting go of anything that would get in the way of seeing what really needs to happen. What you do has to be the right thing, it has to be the intelligent thing. And all of the usual thoughts and feelings that might keep us from taking action when action needs to be taken have to be out of the way. It is not a time for procrastinating.

It's not a time for being overwhelmed, although it would be easy to feel overwhelmed in that kind of situation. It is a time for being present and being clear. It's not a time for objecting, for wishing that this thing hadn't happened, whatever it is. The storm could have been a time of recrimination for me. I knew that bad weather was a possibility— but not like this. The forecast had said that there was a possibility of thunderstorms, but I wasn't thinking of *this* kind of thunderstorm. I could have been lost in self-recrimination, but it wasn't a time for that.

It was fortunate that the storm lasted only about 20 minutes. The waves in Long Island Sound didn't have a chance to build to the level I have sometimes seen. The seas calmed, the sun came out, and it was all over. We were drenched, but it was a warm day. We found out later that a tornado touched down in Bridgeport, and there were gusts of wind in the area that were 78 miles an hour. A state of emergency had been declared.

We had pulled through, with a little damage to the boat. Over the rest of our voyage, there were other things that came up—none so threatening but daily events, as there often are on a sailboat, when steps need to be taken. There are a whole host of bad possible outcomes if you don't do what needs to be done. I suppose that's one of the reasons I like sailing, because it calls a person to action, it calls a person to awareness; it calls one to be present and see what's happening, and then do something about it.

By the time we got to the place where we dry-docked our boat in Delaware Bay, I felt energized. I felt alive in a way I hadn't felt in a long time. I think we felt that together. Our boat, this little 30-foot world, was encompassed, surrounded by our spirit of care. There was life aboard that boat, and just about every part of our little craft had received some attention from us. Most important, life was preserved, and it was bursting through us and our loved ones.

I came home to find that it is wonderful not only to go on a trip and visit strange and new places, but it is wonderful to come home. I have found that I see where I am from in the light of new experiences when I travel, and this was particularly true on this occasion. What I noticed was how many things there are in my world that need attention but which just sit there. There are issues that I just do not address.

It seemed to me that, as human beings, we have come to live a life where we just tolerate things that do not work, that in fact threaten life in some way, that threaten our well-being, that threaten the joy and fulfillment of our life and those around us. There are all the insidious little habits that creep in, all the sense of overwhelm that makes a person say, "What could I do? I'm just one person; it will always be there tomorrow," and so on and so forth. There is nothing like a storm to galvanize a person into action.

It's said that if you take a frog and put it in boiling water, it will jump out immediately. But if you put it in lukewarm water and gradually raise the temperature, there is no point at which the frog realizes that it needs to get out of that pot. I think a human life can go something like that.

So what stops you from doing the thing that you need to do? From saying what you need to say to the people around you, so they can hear you? So they can hear your vision and they can feel the imperative of life that you are feeling and the imperative of action—perhaps so they can feel your blessing and your love?

- What would compel you to embrace a new attitude, if you hold judgments of other people or yourself?

- What would stir you to say, "That's enough!—it is killing me to think all these thoughts, believing this about another person or me, or having this attitude"?

- What stops you when you feel the compulsion to do what you know you are deeply called to do, but sit on it? When you put it off, put it off, and put it off, finding reasons not to act.

Usually, there are things that a person could do to raise the quality of life that they are experiencing—things that could bring greater health, greater happiness, greater service to others, and greater fulfillment. But somehow people forget that. They think it always has to be *this* way. But it could be different—you could take an action that would make it different for you and for the people around you. You could increase the level of vibrancy and joy. How much joy and fulfillment can you stand to have in your life? How about raising the capacity to accept joy, to accept fulfillment?

All too many people have the belief that they have to trudge through life the way they have been. Maybe you could change that and, in a real way, experience something different, experience something more, share more with your friends, and remove some of those ceilings that have been operative in your life. You don't have to go looking for a storm; but if one arises, perhaps it is an opportunity for your victory.

You might know the story of how they train elephants in the East. They put a post in the ground and they chain the baby elephant's foot to the post. The baby elephant tries to move, and it can't. Years go by, and the elephant grows up. It becomes a huge, lumbering beast and still allows itself to be tied to that same post in the ground, believing that it doesn't have the strength and the power to pull it up, to uproot it and do something different.

The larger part of who you are knows that there are limitations that are unnatural to you as a human being. The larger part of you knows that you can take the actions in your life now that preserve life, that bring the deepest joy and greatest fulfillment. You can face the storms that might arise, and meet them with courage and victory.

TRY THIS: *Think of a situation where you have been avoiding action that would preserve an opportunity for something in your life to flourish.*

Close your eyes. Imagine taking that action.

Sense how it feels. Now open your eyes and take that action.

A Practical Spirituality

The world needs a practical spirituality—one that is relevant to the individual challenges that people meet every day and to the largest issues facing humanity. Doesn't it seem to you that many of the religions and spiritual paths offered in the world today rely on a belief in the fantastic? Fantastic ideas about other dimensions, other galaxies, or what happens after you die. If what appears to be fantastic opens the mind to real awareness and experience, it might serve a purpose. I'm not interested in an endless quest for the spiritual experience promoted by someone else, but unavailable to be experienced here and now. The world needs a practical spirituality, and so do you and I.

As the spiritual director of Sunrise Ranch, a center for programs that offer a spiritual experience to people, I find myself welcoming those who are looking for something new in their life. But for the most part, I don't think they are looking for a new cosmology, a new guru, or new beliefs. They are seeking a way to let spirituality become real for them.

Often, to them, Sunrise Ranch seems to be an idyllic place. We are a spiritual community of 100 people. Much of the food we eat is raised right on the property or in the local area. The valley here is full of wildlife. And we have an active program of spiritual practices. So in many ways it is a place set apart from the world. Sunrise Ranch is a special place that offers support for facing the pivotal issues in a person's life. But we do a poor job of helping people to avoid those issues. We usually find that after people have been here for a month or two, they hit a wall. The person living next to them is catty. They don't have enough time to meditate. The work is too hard. The honeymoon is over, and they have the opportunity to rise above and overcome what has been challenging them in their life. They can leave behind the people and circumstances of their prior world, but they have to do something about the state of their own thoughts and feelings. They have to come to terms with the experience they are creating for themselves.

This gets right to the heart of *practical spirituality*. Within everyone, there is an impulse that causes them to desire something wonderful in their life. A superficial spirituality has a person forever seeking that from another person, from a book, or from a spiritual teaching. While all those things can be significant steps along a person's path—perhaps even necessary ones—if they really are steps and not distractions, they lead people to the dreadful, awe-inspiring realization that the wonder they seek is within them, looking to get out. And the only thing really stopping that from happening is themselves.

I had a friend who suffered from anxiety. As far as I could tell, it had no easily identifiable source, either from his environment or from his past. But still, he was plagued by insomnia and other symptoms. There came a time when something changed for him. He began to transform his own experience and share his process with others. He spoke to others about bursting through self-imposed limitations that so many people accept for themselves. He talked about being conscious of the self-deprecating inner critic that most people harbor within themselves. A great spirit of inspiration poured through him to other people, and his experience changed.

It is the creative spirit within us all, looking to get out, that torments us if we don't let it out. I think about the people I hold in high esteem; people like Civil Rights leader Martin Luther King, Jr., South African President Nelson Mandela, and many others. What if they had kept their creative spirit locked up inside? What would Martin Luther King, Jr.'s life been like if he kept the dream he had for the world locked up inside him? I believe he would have been an agonizingly unhappy man. What if Mother Teresa kept her service to the poor of Calcutta locked up inside her? You might say that these great leaders led lives full of strife as they brought their gifts to the world. I say that given the choice between the agony of keeping my spirit locked up inside of me, and the challenge of letting it out, I'll take the latter every time.

Practical spirituality isn't chasing after something wonderful, whether you see that as being spiritual or not. It is staying where you are and letting what is full of wonder find you. And it is letting a world be created—or re-created—because you are willing to be exactly where you are. Practical spirituality is welcoming what is coming to you from within and letting it out, and it is welcoming what is coming to you from without and letting it in.

So how do you welcome what is within you? Creating time and space that welcomes what is within you is a way of acknowledging and honoring that reality. This is the essence of meditation. It is the heart of worship. You honor your own spirit, which is part of the spirit of all, when you give it a place to live and breathe in your awareness. You become a vessel for that spirit, which begins to overflow into the world. You have ceased looking for that experience. You have been willing to be where you are and let your inner reality find you.

You have to create time in your life that is set aside to welcome what is within you. There has to be space for what is within you to flow through your thoughts and feelings—a physical space such as a room or a place in nature, set aside from your usual worldly concerns. But it also has to be an open space in mind and heart that welcomes the fire within you. Within that space, there has to be a wild and radical openness that banishes the pedestrian concerns of life, and with heart-splitting abandon cleaves to the force of nature that is within you.

You have to be willing to be shaken inside by such an encounter. Through it, you are welcoming creative spiritual power into the world— the all-consuming love of who you are, the truth of who you are.

A practical spirituality requires that a person finds a way to continue the experience they have had in times of meditation and worship in the rest of their life. Reflecting on my own experience, and witnessing others, I observe that this isn't always an easy process. What is awakening within a person in times of meditation and worship can't be applied as is, without thought, to the everyday situations of a person's life. It takes care and thoughtful consideration. And it takes faith in the virtue of bursting into action when that is called for.

I imagine that almost everyone who has had an experience of spiritual awakening has tried to share it with their worlds in ways that didn't work well—regaling a family member with impassioned descriptions of what they are experiencing, or trying to be soft and kind in a situation that demanded clarity and precision. But that doesn't mean that the spiritual outpouring established in meditation and worship is irrelevant in a person's life. It just takes conscious thought to see how that outpouring relates to the world you live in and to find creative ways to bring that flow to other people.

A young man applying to a spiritual program I teach came up to me after I gave a talk. He was enthusiastic that I had spoken about the virtue of thinking creatively and then acting on those thoughts. He told me about a spiritual path he had followed where the leaders had taught him that the mind was the cause of people's spiritual downfall, and that you shouldn't think—just believe. Isn't that kind of "spirituality" a recipe for dysfunction? A setup for failure? "You're fine as long as you are meditating, praying, or worshipping. The minute your life causes you to think and to act, you are not being spiritual." We need a practical spirituality that honors the opportunities we have in our human experience.

If a person is serious about a practical spirituality, they undertake this work. *Because what is within you wants out.* It wants to burst into action through you. It wants to bring an answer to all the questions of your life. It wants to bring the enfolding, encompassing properties of love to the people in your world. It wants to stand as you, revealed in all your glory. That is a practical spirituality.

What is the spiritual impulse within you that wants to burst out?
What steps could you take to act on that impulse?

Flipping the Switch

Here is a consciousness exercise for personal empowerment. Imagine that somewhere in the recesses of your consciousness there is a switch. It is not so small as a wall switch or the switch on a computer. This is a big, honking electrical switch with an arm 6 feet long. To be turned on, you have to lift that switch to an upright position until it is seated in the prongs that receive it, metal on metal. When that circuit is closed, high-voltage current comes on and you light up.

Imagine that switch is somewhere deep in the recesses of your mind. You have come across it, and the problem is the arm is down and the circuit is not on. And you have a chance to do something about it.

But here is the challenge. There is a big sign in front of the switch. The letters on the sign say, "You did it." Inherently you know the deeper meaning of the sign. It is that you have created your life experience as it is. Then you see below, in smaller letters, this statement: "You *are* doing it."

There is a large, white pill sitting on the table next to the sign, and you know that to swallow that pill is to accept the message on the sign.

You can imagine, seeing the open switch and then seeing the sign and the pill, there might be some recoil. Being confronted with the idea that your current experience, with whatever suffering might be a part of it, is being created by you, you might think, "I'm getting out of here! I don't want any piece of this. It is just too hard a pill to swallow, to believe that the responsibility for my experience doesn't lie with anyone other than me."

So a timid person would walk away, knowing that it seems to be a lot easier to believe that somebody else did it, or the world did it, or, if you're religious, God did it. Your parents did it—they are easy targets; your school, your government, your teachers, your boss, your . . . whatever did it. There is a certain perverse satisfaction we get out of believing that somebody else made us live our life as it is.

But there is only one problem: as long as we won't swallow that pill and then grab on to that switch and accept the responsibility that we are creating our lives, the circuit isn't closed, and life current is unavailable to us—at least in the magnitude and in the way that it's meant to be for us as human beings. We are not lit up.

Before swallowing this bitter pill of personal responsibility for our life, a person has an experience of victimhood. But there is more to it than victimhood, because if a person feels victimized, they do not want to stay in that condition long; so typically, they try to work life out so that they are not victimized anymore. There might be a sense that they are entitled to something other than victimhood, which is true. So they try to work it out so that what the world, and the people in it, gives them, makes them happy.

This is an attempt to convert the experience of victimhood to one of being a happy consumer, so that the things that are done to a person are good and pleasure producing. People are kinder. More money flows to them. They experience better health. On the face of it, this seems to be a logical approach. There is only one problem. It does not work—at least not for long—if the person has not swallowed the bitter pill. There is always someone or something around that spoils it.

This is not just an individual consideration. Human civilization is largely built around the assumption of victimhood and the attempt to change the experience of victimhood to the experience of being happy consumers. We have structures of commerce, government, and religion, and even spiritual paths that are based in turning ourselves into happy consumers, perhaps even happy consumers of the gifts of God. The problem is that this approach, while so widespread and seemingly so logical, denies who we are as Creator Beings. It omits the role that individuals have in creating their world. It omits the role that we, as humanity, have in creating the world.

So what happens if we are willing to swallow this bitter pill and accept "I did it—I created this life"? We become empowered. We are talking empowerment here, because when you accept responsibility for what you have been doing and what you are creating, you can find out how you could do it differently. You can explore within yourself how you have habitually created the situations in your life. Then, with the current on, you can allow the necessary intensification of life current into your experience that reroutes the whole pattern, in yourself and in your life, that takes that habitual way of thinking and feeling and reorients it.

The life current that runs through our personal circuit can restructure our life. It can repolarize all the patterns and forms of our life. So if you want your life to reshape, you need to bring an intensification of that current. But as long as a person is not taking responsibility for their life, they cannot find the switch. They are wandering around, wondering why their life experience is what it is.

TRY THIS: *Stand up from where you might be sitting. Imagine a shelf before you and on that shelf is a large, white pill that is your acceptance that you are responsible for your life.*

Now swallow it. With that acceptance, step up boldly to the switch.

Imagine that this huge switch is open before you, sitting in a horizontal position.

See the sign between you and the switch saying, "You did it. You are doing it."

Using your inherent strength, lift that switch until it is fully upright and engaged.

Feel the current of your empowering life choice surge through your body, from your toes all the way up through you.

This power will reshape your life if you let it continue to flow. It will take courage to face the heretofore hidden ways you have been choosing to live your life as you do. With that insight comes the opportunity to choose to create it differently.

Is this not real freedom? The freedom to be ourselves. The freedom to act as the creator of our life. The freedom to shape our world in the most creative way possible.

Heaven's Champion

He is our champion
With flaming, golden hair,
And the courage of young David in his heart.

He goes for us
As the gates of hell open
And every ghost and demon
Of the human heart
Is unleashed by the children of men.

He stands in the heat of noon
When the sun sits high in the cloudless sky,
With a blaze of glory on his brow,
And waits quietly in the cool of the day,
To watch, to listen;
To bow before his Lord.

A choir of angels sings through his words,
Heaven's light, his eyes,
And his presence fills the air,
Like love's dew at the first sunrise.
Yes, he is our champion,
Our fair-haired one,

And so much more—
Our beloved, our friend,
The emissary
Who goes in our name.
Blessed is he.

Feminine and Masculine Facets of the Warrior Archetype

A practical spirituality requires that people be aware of the quality of energy they are bringing into the world, and also be aware of what is happening energetically in the people around them. Almost everyone has the innate ability to perceive the human energy field around them. Often, that perceptive ability is buried in the subconscious somewhere and the individual loses track of what they intuitively know. So it is a rare person who has cultivated that awareness so that he or she is consciously perceptive of what is actually occurring.

Practical spirituality invites us to be conscious, to be willing to be aware, and to work consciously with the energetic context in which we live. It invites us to be aware of the spiritual commons in which we are functioning—the *spiritual* commons, not just the physical space held in common, although that is part of the picture. Not just the mental commons, the commons of ideas, but the spiritual commons, where the quality of energy, the quality of spirit that people are bringing, is seen to be the ultimate currency, the real moving element that shapes what is happening in our world.

We are called to be powerful people energetically in that commons. To be a powerful person in our world is the work of the spiritual warrior. At the physical level, the warrior's work can be translated as violence, and certainly it has been. This planet's history is filled with conquering, domination, and all kinds of awful things. So we know full well where warrior energy can go.

You might know for yourself where your own warrior energy can go. You might know the damage that you can do. Even if you have not conquered a nation or enslaved an ethnic group, you might have dominated a person in an unhealthy and unkind way. If you have done that, you might have told yourself, "I will never do that again. I hate myself for doing that."

Still, it is natural for us to be strong people in our world. So in some way we have to deal with our strength. We can choose to be unconscious of it. We can try to be small. Have you ever tried to do that? Have you ever thought, "I'll just go away and be small, and maybe things will work better"? How long can you keep that up?

The choice is to either find a noble use of your strength or to be weak.

You might know what it could look like to be a physical warrior. Or perhaps a mental warrior with dominating ideas. What would it mean to be a true spiritual warrior?

There is a feminine way to be a warrior and there is a masculine way to be a warrior. I do not mean that it is only women who engage the feminine way, or just men who engage the masculine way. Each of us possesses masculine and feminine qualities that we call on in different situations. For instance, a man can be loving and nurturing to his children, and a woman can be a jet fighter pilot. The feminine way of being a spiritual warrior is to protect sacred space. The feminine dynamic of the spiritual warrior says, "This space here—*my* space, *my* home, *my* family, *my* organization, is precious to me. And anything or anyone that would come into this space that would spoil it or harm the people in this space is *not* welcome."

That is the spirit of the feminine warrior who protects and keeps sacred what ought to be protected and kept sacred. And why? So that the sacred process of creation may continue. So that the inhabitant of the space, and the living processes of it, are kept safe and thrive. That is the dynamic of the feminine spiritual warrior.

We have a lot of reason to feel shame over this dynamic of the masculine warrior because of the history of humanity. You can think about your own history and the history of your people. My own father's family was Jewish, and if I read the stories of the ancient Hebrews, they were a warring, conquering people, and I certainly do not want to be that kind of person.

I live in the United States, and part of my family is from Kentucky, dating back to the early settlers. I feel shame for what we did as a people to the Native Americans who were present when my ancestors first came to this country. It was shameful. And I am sorry that my country and my ancestors enslaved black people and brought them from Africa to our country and treated them horribly. It too was a shameful thing.

You can think about what it is for your background. I have friends of European descent who live in South Africa. I notice that they feel the burden of the history of apartheid. And if you are from a European background, it is not just South Africa where injustice has been done. There has been political and economic imperialism around the world.

While there has been some noble character in all of that, there has also been domination and barbarism. And the same is true for many other cultures around the world, whether it is Japan, the United States, or somewhere else. A person with this kind of history might be reluctant to allow the archetype of the warrior to fully emerge in their own experience—even if it was the *spiritual* warrior who had an altogether different purpose and premise for the use of their innate strength.

The masculine dynamic of the spiritual warrior is the extension of spiritual energy into the spiritual commons in which the warrior finds himself. It is a contribution to the spiritual commons. In the masculine dynamic, you realize you can bring a profound creative influence into the world that is not just in your space. It is not just for you and yours. Your strength as a spiritual warrior can serve a larger and larger field. You are bigger than your home. Your nature is to be expansive. You are destined to increase your ambit—your sphere of creative influence—into greater fields. Your nature is to bring the dominion of love into an ever-increasing world of influence—into the spiritual commons.

How far does your influence rightly extend? To explore this question, consider what you care about. How big is that? Your family? Your friends? Your organization or community? Your nation? You may be aware that you will not be happy unless this whole world is healthy and whole. You may become aware that your own destiny and fulfillment are not separate from the well-being of this whole world. Your creative influence extends as far as your care.

Your spirit is intrinsically tied to what is happening all over this world. You can choose not to be aware of it, but it matters to you what is happening around this world. You will feel it. If there is a hardship in Australia or in China, you feel it. When nuclear power plants in Japan leak, your world is affected. When something happened on 9/11 in New York City, people felt it around the world. Why? Because it was happening in their spiritual domain. Because, in truth, we are that large.

It is hard to burst toward what you care about without owning the dimensions of your own spiritual warrior. If you do not own that, you might be playing small. Owning your capacity as a spiritual warrior, you come to see that you are a person of great stature, and that extends at least to the four corners of the Earth. Your destiny is not to be a victim of what happens in this world. You are the spiritual warrior who changes the world.

TRY THIS: *Think of a situation where you are being called to own your own spiritual warrior. What is it that you are being called to do?*

Critical Mass

How do you achieve critical mass for fusion for the creative field in which you work? That creative field has many dimensions to it. It is the physical space in which you live, including your own body. It is the network of relationships you have with other people. It is the money that flows through your bank account, and it is the projects you undertake. We reach critical mass when we have manifested a viable, growing energetic form in the middle of our creative field. The critical mass is not the form alone but also the dynamism of that form. There is a time in the life of every creative field for critical mass to be attained; a time when the creative power that is bursting through that field—and everyone in it—has to be embraced.

The pivotal factor in reaching critical mass for the creative field you inhabit is consciousness. Consciousness is pivotal because changes there change the rest of the field. It is through shifts in consciousness that a critical mass of creative energy can be achieved that transforms the entire field.

Perhaps the easiest place to see how critical mass can be achieved is in relationship to this book. You are one of many people who will read these words. Up until now, you might have thought of yourself as a single person having your own unique experience. You might have given little thought to all the other readers who are having their own unique experience. These individuals live on six continents around the world. Geographically speaking, they are a widely disparate set of people, most of whom are separated by vast distances over land and sea, feeling little association with one another.

Spend a few moments thinking about these people. Imagine them, wherever they might be, contemplating the same ideas that you have been contemplating as you have been reading. They are different from you in many ways, but they are also the same. They have your interest in building a sun. They have so many of the same human experiences that you have. So while you could think of them as isolated people around the globe, these are people who are linked together by a common interest and passion.

They are together with one another and with you in aspiring to have a deeper understanding of their life and a deeper spiritual attunement. As they read this chapter in the book, they are thinking about you and all the other readers. And just because you live on Planet Earth with them, you share a common destiny. If you have children, your children and their children will be inheriting the world together.

Relative to the field of consciousness and energy that you share with the readers of this book, open your thoughts to what could happen if the potential of that field were fulfilled as completely as possible. You could meet some of those people and collaborate with them to accomplish something creative and wonderful. What if the most glorious thing that could occur actually did occur with them? Let yourself feel the feelings that are associated with that glorious thing. What you will likely find is that as you let yourself experience this, your energy field changes. Your energy field has transformed. It has begun to be the means by which the potential of this creative field could manifest in form.

In any creative field there are many factors that can lead people to experience themselves as separate, and therefore prevent critical mass. You might have different ideas and beliefs than other people. And even the concern that you *could* have different ideas and beliefs can keep you separate from others. You might have an aversion to being close personally or emotionally to other people. You might have an aversion to being close to certain kinds of people. Or you might consider yourself an independent person—not a joiner.

Perhaps more important than anything else, you might never have thought of the possibility that there could be critical mass achieved by the people in your creative field, just as you might have never thought of that possibility relative to those who read this book. There are many factors in consciousness that create a paradigm of separateness. Those divisive factors can be the defining feature of consciousness, and therefore the defining feature of the creative field. You can change the paradigm. You can hold the possibility that the people in your field will come together dynamically to bring life to that field. You cannot make it happen. But as you are a sun, you are bringing the warmth, the light, and the gravity that brings life.

In the process, you are healing a wound in consciousness. That wound is separateness. As we ourselves experience critical mass—a coming together in thought and feeling, and a great flow of spiritual energy—the wound is healed. Healing the wound of separateness in our immediate creative field, we create a critical mass of consciousness. We take a step toward healing the wound of separateness in the body of humanity. Critical mass is gravity at the center of the creative field, drawing to itself the substance that is uniquely suited to play its part in the field. The people that are right for that field. The money that is needed. The resources. All made possible because you have seen your field as whole, and you are giving birth to God the Manifest.

TRY THIS:

Think about a situation where you are keeping yourself separate.

What can you do to close the gap that separates you from a person, a cause, or an organization? Are you ready to take a step toward closing that gap?

We Will Open

We will open those hidden portals
In the flesh
Which let this stellar light
Penetrate, at last
Those darkened corners
Of this grand, human obstinacy.

O, yes, we will,
My dear companion,
We shall bring our simple answer
To this worldly fraud,
The preposterous travesty
Of a feigned human life.

And we will tell our souls,
And the souls of all men,
And all women,
To truly live,
To breathe,
And forget the ancient sadness
That assails the human heart.

O, yes, dear one,
We will live and breathe,
And bring beauty
To every corner of our Being,
And as we do,
To every sea,
Every land,
To the four directions of this world,
And ask, for our Creator . . .

"Will you open now
To that spirit who you are?
Will you forsake now your hardened ways?
Will you now embrace
With your every cell and gland and tissue,
That power who made you,
That creative energy,
That being,
That flaming spark
Who is your God?

"Will you now?"

"Can you now?"
Yes, you can.

And you will be held
In heaven's love,
As the light of the stars
Enters each earthly door,
Opening you
To the sacred reality
Of your inmost Being.

Fully Entering Your Life

In Shakespeare's *Henry V*, Act 4, Scene 3, this is addressed to the king on the brink of the Battle of Agincourt in the year 1415:

> *O that we now had here*
> *But one ten thousand of those men in England*
> *That do no work to-day!*

Have you ever had such a thought? "Sure do wish there were more people helping me!"

Here is the king's reply, known as the St. Crispin's Day speech:

> *This story shall the good man teach his son;*
> *And Crispin Crispian shall ne'er go by,*
> *From this day to the ending of the world,*
> *But we in it shall be remember'd;*
> *We few, we happy few, we band of brothers;*
> *For he to-day that sheds his blood with me*
> *Shall be my brother; be he ne'er so vile,*
> *This day shall gentle his condition:*
> *And gentlemen in England now-a-bed*
> *Shall think themselves accursed they were not here,*
> *And hold their manhoods cheap whiles any speaks*
> *That fought with us upon Saint Crispin's day.*

The spiritual journey is often spoken of as a battle. I have no interest in shedding my blood or the blood of anyone else. But I do love the passion of this speech. And I have no idea what others will think in the days to come about what I am doing now. I know that I am here to do what is mine with those who will do it with me. Do you share that passion?

It can be an awesome thought to realize that what you do, or do not do, makes a great difference to the outcome of something that is important to you. People often dread that awareness and avoid it. It is far easier to think that what other people do will make the difference, or that powerful leaders in far-off places are determining what will happen in your creative field. It is much more comfortable to think that, or at least it seems so.

If you are associated with an organization of some kind, it is far easier, it seems, to think that what the leadership of that organization does is what is really going to make the difference in your life. Or that the *culture* of the organization, which is more nebulous than the leadership, is the most influential factor in what is important. It might be easy to think such things, but it is personally disempowering.

What you do or do not do will make a great difference to the outcome of something that is important to you, and the process of spiritual evolution includes coming to terms with that realization. It includes taking on the apparent burden of responsibility for things you care about. It can seem like such a heavy burden.

A real spiritual journey leads you to come to terms with your own tendency to shirk that responsibility and to project it on other people. It leads you to come to terms with your own dread of being a slave to what you care about—your dread that you could be woken up at any hour of the day or night in service to what you hold as important, or that you could be called on to burst into action—which, if you had not taken on the burden of what you care about, you might not otherwise have had to do.

The spiritual journey is about taking on this, which appears to be a burden, and finding that it is the greatest joy and fulfillment of your life. The spiritual journey takes a person to a higher and higher experience of God the Possible. But that experience becomes meaningless to a person unless they commit themselves to be the means by which what is possible manifests in their world.

The sacred Hindu scripture, the Bhagavad-Gita, speaks of the spiritual journey as a battle. It begins on the eve of war with this exhortation, spoken by Krishna to Arjuna in Chapter 2:

How hath this weakness taken thee?
Whence springs
The inglorious trouble, shameful to the brave,
Barring the path of virtue? Nay, Arjuna!
Forbid thyself to feebleness! it mars
Thy warrior-name! cast off the coward-fit!
Wake! Be thyself! Arise, Scourge of thy Foes!

The battle is a metaphor for a person's willingness to fully enter their life, with all the confrontation, risk, and opportunity that life contains. A person enters the battle when they accept that they, themselves, are central to manifesting what they really care about.

When a person begins to come to terms with their own power to make a difference in their world, it is daunting. Often, at first, they believe that they are all alone or greatly outnumbered as they take responsibility for manifesting what is important to them. The spiritual journey gives us the opportunity to confront that limiting belief. It is learning to participate in the process by which what is a potential actually manifests. It includes the realization that no one will ever join us in manifesting what we care about unless we engage in that process ourselves.

I have had to face these issues in my life. There was a time, in 2004, when I assumed responsibility for leading Sunrise Ranch and Emissaries of Divine Light, when it looked like almost all my friends were leaving me—people who I thought were necessary to the work that I was doing. People I loved and admired left me. People who had strong professional skills found that there were other activities that were more important for them. It looked really bleak.

Fortunately, my heart would not let me stop what I was doing. As I continued, I found that there were people who wanted to do the work with me. And so our work has flourished over the years. More and more people have come to share in what we are building and to lend their strength to the effort.

When you come to terms with these issues on your spiritual path, you have the opportunity to manifest the greatest potential for your world. And when you manifest in form the essence of what is precious to you, it is glorious. What greater pleasure and fulfillment is there than seeing what you love and treasure take form and thrive?

A person who commits themselves to what they love in this way has to face the risk that others might not support them in their efforts. What they are attempting might not be successful. They have to confront whatever it is that might stop them from carrying through with their efforts. But even if, for whatever reason, they fall short of what they have worked toward, they will live with the peace that comes from serving what is most important to them.

When you have done your best, when you have given all that is yours to give, when you have taken the action that is yours to take, how things turn out is how they turn out, and what other people do is what other people do, whatever it is. You have done your part in seeing something all the way through. You have done your part in manifesting what is potential for the world.

What is the burst of action you are now ready to take?
Is there an impulse inside you that is calling for your expression
into the world?

Chapter Four

THE FUSION

OF

FULFILLING MISSION

A small body of determined spirits fired by an unquenchable faith in their mission can alter the course of history.

~ MOHANDAS GANDHI ~

Your Life Matters

On a clear night, where I live in Colorado, we have a view of endless stars. Seeing the Milky Way, the Pleiades, Orion, and all the other celestial bodies, I can feel the vastness of being on a scale that I cannot wrap my mind around.

We are surrounded by the infinite—infinite space, infinite stars, and infinite potential for this human life. It stretches in all directions.

We are surrounded by the eternal—time before all beginnings, reaching beyond all endings.

The nature of your life as a human being is to be present here and now in this moment in time, in this immediate place where you are reading these words. The infinite and the eternal are present with you in this place—all those stars, solar systems, and galaxies, and all that space. All those eons of time that have led to this moment—your parents' parents' parents, and so many generations before them. The unfoldment of all creation before the first human being. And all the unfolding kaleidoscope of infinite possible outcomes that are before you in your own life that stretch into future generations of humanity and beyond.

This is what it is like to be a human being. We are endowed with the inheritance of all that has led up to this moment and with all that has come to us from the infinite universe. This is our legacy. It has taken it all to bring us to this point.

Our destiny lies before us. That destiny is composed of the moments, days, and years of our own life to come. It is also the larger destiny of our children, our species, and of Planet Earth and beyond, reaching into the eternal unfoldment of creation.

All that has gone before is present with you now. All the future is present in seed form with you now. So what will you do? You are made as a human being to receive the legacy of the past and the influence of the infinite and to sow the seeds of the future. You live at the confluence of all that has been and what will be. Your life depends on it. All those who come after you depend on it. What you think and say and do now matters.

This is what it is like to be a human being. It is glorious to live in the dynamic between the spiritual and the earthly, in which your full presence in this immediate time and place is a fulfillment of the vastness of the spiritual. This is the dynamic between the fire of the sun that you are and the earth of your being. Creation can continue because you show up as the sun in your life. How it continues depends on you.

If the vastness of the infinite and the eternal were just energy and matter, it might not matter so much what happened to it in your life.

But the truth is that there is so much more to creation than that. There are people involved, and people are precious. The lives of all those who came before you matter. All they did that lets you be here now matters. If any of your ancestors did not live their life, you could not be here as you are now today. There are so many who have given so much to let you be here now. And just as you receive the benefit of all who have gone before you, people in your life and those who come after you receive the benefit of your life.

But it is not just the people in your life who give it meaning. They are not the only part of creation that is alive. The infinite and the eternal are not just energized stuff. They are not just energy and matter. They are full of what people are full of—Universal Being. Perhaps it is easier to see that reality in people. We are clearly not just *something*. We are *someone*. There is selfhood.

All of creation is like that. It is not just *something*. It is *someone*. The animals, rocks, trees, and stars are alive. They are Universal Being embodied in living form. That is why creation is so beautiful and so precious. All that has come to you has been a gift of Universal Being given to you now in this present moment. That awareness is the difference between being dead inside and being truly alive.

Just as a cloudy night obscures the light of the stars, clouds in consciousness can obscure the infinite and the eternal. Worries about the future can dominate thoughts and feelings. Grief about the past can haunt people, and anger can consume them. Because of these clouds in consciousness, people can lose touch with the vastness around them and feel trapped in their immediate surroundings. They can forget their connection with that vast reality.

You are fulfilled as you remember that your life in this world is in service to Universal Being—to the people who came before you and to those who follow after you, to your own being, your own self, and to the Universal Being of all creation. The infinite and the eternal, which is your inheritance, is the reality of Universal Being. The infinite possibility that is before you is your opportunity to participate in Universal Being as an embodiment of that reality, to give the gift that is yours to give so that creation can continue, unbroken through you.

It takes a celestial opening to truly embrace this knowing, this experience. This is what allows you to fulfill your mission in life as a human being. As you do, you are serving what you love and value. You are honoring Universal Being. The universe is empowering you to act.

Through the creative magic of reciprocity, you are fusing with what you love and serve. You are growing beyond an experience of being a person in dedicated service to something you love, to an experience of knowing that you are Universal Being in living form. You are becoming a sun.

So what will you do? Will you do your part as a fully awake and fully present human being? Will you let your physicality serve your spirituality? Or will you try to pretend that the beingness of other people, of you, and of all creation does not matter? The universe awaits your answer.

What are the opportunities you have to become more deeply in touch with the vastness around you? Are there clouds of anger, fear, or grief that are in the way?

Commission

Ever since I was young, I knew I had something great to do in this world. The stories my mother read to me as a boy—of Robin Hood, King Arthur, and Ulysses—fired my imagination; stories of standing up to the sheriff of Nottingham, of facing the deceit of Morgan le Fay, and challenging the thievery and betrayal of Paris of Troy called me to do something great myself.

Sailing adventures with my father as a 10-year-old confirmed my childhood experience that life was thrilling. With my younger brother, Peter, we took a two-week cruise from Westport, Connecticut, to Gardiner's Bay on the other end of Long Island Sound in an 18-foot sloop. The climax of the trip was a storm with 11-foot seas. My father stripped the sails down to the jib. We surfed the seas back to Port Jefferson on Long Island, my brother and I gleeful as we slid down each gray, mountainous wave.

It was this sense of the thrill and greatness of life that collided with the world as I saw it as a 16-year-old. This is what led me to search for an alternative to the life I saw in front of me—to the dreariness of school and the possibility of service in an unjust war in Vietnam. It was what fired my interest in alternative community at a kibbutz in Israel and then at a commune in Maine.

I understand now that I was looking for my mission—for what had called to me since I was a boy reading those stories. I had a high capacity to commit myself to a great purpose. But it had to be a mission that commanded my honor and respect. It had to be real and true.

My first trip to Sunrise Ranch was in the summer of 1975, immediately after graduating from university. I took a three-month spiritual program with four classroom hours in the morning and work on the Ranch in the afternoon. I loved the haying operation, stacking bales on the trailer moving through the fields. The hay scratched my forearms and the dust got up in my nostrils. But I loved it. The hard work, the camaraderie among the men, and the outdoors all fed my soul.

The goal of the spiritual education was to develop the participant's ability to be an attunement server—someone who could assist another to find an experience of attunement with the source of life within them. I was 22 years old at the time and I was loving it.

Two months into the program, I had the strangest perception. It came upon me during a picnic supper by the pool with the participants, faculty, and staff. As I gazed about at the people around me, it seemed to me that I was about to become the leader of Sunrise Ranch. And not only the leader of Sunrise Ranch, but the leader of Emissaries of Divine Light, for which Sunrise Ranch was the headquarters.

Why would I even imagine this? I'm the youngest person in the program.
Most participants are at least 10 years older than me,
which is like a lifetime.
The leaders of Sunrise Ranch are between two and three times my age.
I am fresh out of college. Why would this even cross my mind?

It was like a daydream—an alternate reality that was superimposed on my daily experience of the Ranch. After living with this strange perception that was haunting my thoughts for several days, I dismissed it.

Seriously, David, that doesn't make any sense, I told myself and put it on the shelf in a back closet of my mind, where it would sit for decades. I focused my attention on the teachings and on the hay, accepting the opportunities that arose for me, day to day.

As the years went by, the commitment to my mission took the form of commitment to people around me who were leading projects that I deemed important. They received my love and my service.

In 2002, I found myself leading with two other men at Sunrise Ranch. One of them was a gifted executive leader and the other carried a burning passion for Sunrise Ranch and everything for which it stood. I was devoted to each of them. In fact, I had moved to Sunrise Ranch from Connecticut two years earlier to support them in their work. I was committed to what we were doing together, and I was committed to supporting each of them to lead us to the fulfillment of our mission as a community.

By February 2004, one of these men had pulled back from his leadership at Sunrise Ranch. The other had told me he was called to move to another country. My heart was sinking. I knew that our organization required leadership that was focused, passionate, and committed.

In fact, it needs a body of leaders who are in solidarity with the mission and with one another, I thought to myself as I considered the impact of these men leaving. I could not see how that would happen without individuals stepping forward. And the people I thought most capable of doing that were not.

With the seven other trustees of Emissaries of Divine Light, I attended our regular biannual meeting in British Columbia. To my surprise, they asked me to lead the organization. It was not unanimous, and it was with conditions. But they asked me to lead. I had devoted myself to being a servant of this organization. At this point in my life, I had not seen myself as leading it and I had forgotten the awareness that I had in my twenties.

In August 2004, I was officially appointed the interim leader of the Emissaries of Divine Light. As soon as I was, several of the trustees and others with whom I was leading felt threatened. I was challenged by them night and day. It felt gut-wrenching to me, as if there was a knife in my belly that was twisted with every doubting comment and every cynical e-mail. I reached out. I begged for understanding. I searched my own soul, trying to see what I might be doing wrong.

In September 2005, my leadership commission was renewed, again on an interim basis. The cynicism and challenge from some of the people closest to me continued to June 2006. Some of the trustees were talking about appointing me to a third year of interim leadership. To me, the interim status was becoming a vote of *no confidence* that gave me no real mandate to lead. I wrote to the trustees, saying this:

It seems to me that the root of the energetic pattern is a difficulty acknowledging and supporting a focus of leadership. Some might say this is about me—about my style versus that of others—but I suspect with someone else in the position the pattern would have surfaced in some way. As it is me, it has come in this way and I don't think it is realistic to assume that I, by myself, can somehow change it or that it will just spontaneously dissolve all on its own . . .

Here is what I propose to do. If I am asked to provide the focus of leadership for this ministry, I will ask that I be given the acknowledgment and support of every trustee to do that job. If the vote, or whatever we do at the end of our review, is not unanimous, I will ask those who would have preferred a different outcome to stay in the container and support me wholeheartedly. I will not in any way hold back my willingness to work with them just because they would have preferred a different outcome. If the majority of the trustee group recommends that I am asked to provide the focus of leadership and any of you cannot support me in that wholeheartedly, I will ask those people to step out of the trustee container, and I will ask for the support of the trustees in making that request. And I imagine that if someone were not keen to work with the recommended direction they would want to step out anyway.

Last, from a personal standpoint, I have gotten clear for myself what I want to create and to participate in. I am interested in living in a surround of love. I want to fulfill my commission in that surround, and I believe that I jeopardize that fulfillment if I hold to myself a surround that is something other than love. I believe that is true of each of you, of the people who participate in this ministry, and of the people who we touch, and that if I and we do not create a surround of love in this, our ultimate circle of leadership, our chances of creating that surround elsewhere in this Emissary program are greatly diminished. I don't experience much of this loving surround in our circle, and I want that to change. I know that the joy and creation that is possible to us all, individually and together, will appear easily if the surround of love is present.

Love always,
David

In September 2006, I was appointed the spiritual director of Emissaries of Divine Light with no interim status attached. I continue in that position today. My service in that role is at the pleasure of the trustees and it is reviewed annually. I continue as one of seven trustees. It has become a constellation of people where love is known.

I have come to embrace my commission—my own special place in the reality of all Being, the character that is unique to me, and the incarnational mission that is mine. I would wish that for anyone.

It was not until several years later that I remembered my strange perceptions in the program I attended at Sunrise Ranch in 1975. I see them now as some kind of premonition—a prophesy of things to come that entered my awareness. I believe that many people have such perceptions. How confusing! To become aware of a potential whose day has not yet come.

This is a story of embracing destiny, calling, and commission. It's also a story of friction and fusion. In my story, there are other people who played a part, and some of them created friction on my journey. To this day, I have respect and appreciation for all the others involved, even though I wished they had made different choices at the time.

But this story is not really about them. It is about me. My destiny. My calling. The fusion of my prior knowing that I was meant to lead, all of the service I had given myself to and the skills I had developed, and the opportunity that had unfolded before me. This story is also about the fusion of the people who did gather around me to fulfill their own calling with me. It is about rising to the occasion when destiny calls. And about honoring that destiny and honoring yourself when that time comes. Your story is about you. Never forget it.

I believe that every human being is called to greatness and that life is a thrill if we are in service to our calling, and from my own experience I would recommend this. Do not deny any premonition of your destiny. And do not try to impose a prophesy of the future on your life now. Give it an honored place in your heart, knowing that a true prophesy will bend the world of the manifest to itself over time. Meanwhile, external events do not define our calling. They do not establish the commission we receive from the Invisible. Whatever happens around you, you can honor that calling, that commission. Embrace it. It means everything to you. It is you, being a sun in your world. And when the time comes for you to lead, step up. Ask for what you need. Shine.

The Calling

From the starlit inner realms of Being,
I speak of unfolding beauty,
Timeless reality,
And the opportunity that arrives new born with the morning sun.
I evoke remembrance
Of your deepest calling,
Your truest reality,
And your cosmic place
Here and now,
Holding this cycle of creation.

From out of the whirlwind,
At the center of creation,
I speak.
I am the peaceful center of Being.
I am stillness in the midst of the turning world,
At rest and assured,
In the middle of the human drama.
I am your strength because I am constant and unmoving in my love.
I am your wisdom because I am the reality you seek.
I am your blessing, to be received by you and given to your world.

I am calling to you even now
From the unseen.
Closer to you than the breath you take.
In dreams and thoughts, I come,
In your restless urge
That will never settle for the trinkets
Of the world.
Hear me now as I say this one thing to you.
Take your place.
Take your place.
Be where you belong
In thought,
In feeling,
In awareness,
In answering the calling of your life,
The calling of the reality you are,
And which you serve.

    Join me, dear one,
    At the center of the storm,
    Inside the clamor and the noise,
    Cloaked in my love,
    Bathed in my peace,
    Overflowing with my joy.
    You belong here.
    And from here
    You may bring
    The transforming, uplifting power
    Of the whirlwind
    Into the phenomenal world.

Remember now,
Remember now,
Your place in this home among the stars,
You were not put here by accident
On this blue-green orb,
The third planet from the sun.
You and your friends made her,
And are restoring her now,
Beginning with her crowning creation,
Man and woman
Made in the image and likeness of who you are.

The morning stars shout for joy!

Fire in the Belly

Fire in the belly is the motivation and empowerment for action. The phrase portrays the dynamic between the spiritual and the physical in human experience. Fire is a symbol for the cosmic force that burns in the spiritual aspect of your human capacity. The belly is synonymous with the physical aspect of your human capacity that embodies the cosmic force symbolized by Earth.

If you ever find that you are lacking motivation in your life, check this dynamic. Ask yourself if the actions you are taking physically are in service to your spirituality. These two aspects of your human capacity— the physical and the spiritual—are present as long as you are alive. But they might not be connected; and if they are not, the dynamic between them is dampened.

Mind and emotion are the components of consciousness that are the connection between the physical and the spiritual. So your thinking and feeling can connect your physical experience—what you are doing and saying in the world—with the spiritual, instead of separating your physical experience from it. When you have a clear awareness of the spiritual, you are empowered by the fire that comes from your fusion with that reality and you have the motivation to act. Your devoted service to the infinite and eternal reality within all Creation gives you fire in the belly. Consciousness is God the Means that connects God the Possible— the spiritual aspect of your experience—with God the Manifest, which is embodied in your physical experience.

To make this connection, you only have to become conscious of the role your actions have in embodying, celebrating, and protecting what you love. You have to let the fire of your Being burn away whatever clouds might be in consciousness that are preventing the sun from shining on the earth of your being. Those clouds are formed from thinking and feeling that has become distracted with the events in physical reality to the extent that there is a loss of awareness of the spiritual. The simple act of turning thought and feeling to what you love allows the earth of your being to catch fire with that love.

The solution to the clouds in consciousness that create low motivation—no fire in the belly—is to regularly think about what is worthy of your highest love and to feel the feelings that go along with those thoughts. Let it fill your mind. Let it fill your feelings. Celebrate it in your words. Write poems and love songs that adore it. Paint pictures that portray it to the eyes. Let your whole life be lived as an ode to what you love.

So what is it that deserves your highest love? Creation is filled with many lovely things and many lovely people. All forms of creation are filled with the mystery and wonder of Universal Being from within. Of themselves, the forms are dust without that mystery and wonder. But the forms can be a window to the Universal Being that comes to life through them. In a unique and magnificent way, human beings can be a personification of Universal Being. All Creation is lovable because it is manifesting Universal Being.

When the clouds are burned away from your consciousness, the forms of creation are a window to the Creator, who is within them. They are a window to heaven.

The Koran 2:164 expresses it this way:

Verily, in the creation of the heavens and of the earth and the succession of night and day and in the ships that speed through the sea with what is useful to man: and in the waters which God sends down from the sky, giving life thereby to the earth after it has been lifeless, and causing all manner of living creatures to multiply thereon; and in the change of the winds, and the clouds that run their appointed courses between sky and earth: [in all this] there are messages indeed for a people who use their reason.

As an imam (an Islamic spiritual leader) once explained to me, the Arabic word *ayah* refers to anything in form that creates an open window through which one can receive these messages. Everyday experiences of life can create a transparent window to an inner reality. And for a man, the most open window is a woman, and for a woman, the most open window is a man.

Could it be true for you that the embodiment of Universal Being in form is what deserves your highest love? Understanding that any form is temporary. It is for a certain cycle in time. And while we might imagine that Universal Being is embodied in form in places other than where we are here and now, what is relevant for us is the way it is, or can be, embodied where we are.

Think about the embodiment of Universal Being that you hold dear. For me, I hold dear the damp Connecticut woods where I grew up. The mountains of Colorado, where I now live, and the abundant wildlife within them. This is a planet of unspeakable beauty. There are the people who are so dear to me in my home at Sunrise Ranch. And all the amazing people I meet around the world.

Welcome your own thoughts and feelings as who and what you love fills them to overflowing. Let your gratitude rise and rise. Now focus on what it is about those people and those things that you love. For instance, think about times when the inner reality of someone you know really fused with the physical reality in an exceptional way. Think about a time when you entered the magic of creation around you in a deep and significant manner.

There is the divine feminine within all Creation. She has been called by many names: Gaia, Mother Nature, Mother Mary, the Goddess, and many more. She is Sophia, who is wisdom; and Aphrodite, who is love. She is the queen of heaven and earth. She is made flesh in every woman, even though her reality might be distorted by clouded consciousness. She is embodied in all Creation. Who wouldn't love and serve her? Who would not protect her? Who would not celebrate her being in all her forms and embody her in their life?

The divine masculine is within all Creation and he has many names: Jesus, Krishna, Buddha, Adonai, Prince of Peace, and Lord of Love. He is within all people and within all Creation, and made flesh in every man, even though his reality might be distorted by clouded consciousness. Who wouldn't serve him with their life? Who wouldn't love and honor his Being and his presence? Who would not foster, love, and protect the embodiment of his Being through human beings anywhere, however it occurs? Who wouldn't honor his reality in their own presence in this world, so that all people and all Creation could feel that presence through you?

The divine feminine and the divine masculine are two realities of Universal Being that come to life in Creation. Meditating deeply on these realities inspires us. There is a wonderful woman, Julia Butterfly Hill, who came to Sunrise Ranch for the 2013 Arise Festival. She is a loving, uplifting presence. When someone tells her that she inspires them, she responds with this question: "To do what?"

We are in service to whatever it is that we give our highest love. What is your highest love? What are you serving? How are you manifesting that service in action? Real service is embodied in what we do. If it is not, it is only an idea or an emotion.

Fire in the belly comes when the clouds clear in consciousness and thoughts and feelings fill with our highest love, and our love is so overwhelming to us that we cannot help but live our life in service to it. For real. On Earth. Through our words and deeds.

What is the fire in your belly calling you to do?
What's at risk to live that passion in your life?

My Love Is Long

My love is long
like this path in front of me,
with blind turns
around sandstone bluffs
and endless switchbacks
that climb to unknown places;
and like a young man
who would walk
such a mountain path,
enjoying the sweat
dripping down his torso,
thirsting for a gaze
from the yet distant peak.

O, yes, my love is long,
and it would climb that way
today,
tomorrow,
and for so many tomorrows to come,
until this earthly frame
could walk no more,

and the spirit of my love
walks on alone,
like a rustling wind,
a shimmering and a flickering
that could do naught else but continue
until I reach the end and aim
of all my climbing;
until I know
my hunger is complete,
at least for now,
that I have loved you
with every hidden part,
all given,
all consumed in living flame
until love alone continues,
informing all its wondrous shapes and colors with itself,
dancing and laughing free.

The Sacred Veil

All life is sacred. Within all people, all nature, all Creation, the sacred is present.

Sacredness is impossible to define. But you know it when you experience it; when you see something so exquisitely beautiful that it takes your breath away. It evokes profound respect and radical amazement. You sense the wholeness and the beingness of someone or something. And you see with different eyes the perfection within the imperfection of life.

In the experience of the sacred you see the pattern of creation—the genius and beauty behind it. And you sense that you are part of that pattern. You also feel keenly all of your human experience that has lost contact with that reality.

Touching the sacred, it is easy to see that there has been a veil that has hidden the experience of it from human beings. People long to experience it. They sacrifice much to catch even a glimpse of it through religion and spirituality, through art and through nature. Consciousness is the veil. Thought and feeling, the dual channels of awareness through which a person receives the sacred into experience, can somehow block it. So instead of a clear reception of the awareness of the sacred, they can bring unending static—a self-generated din of disturbance that obscures it, much like a dark thundercloud obscures the sun.

Imagine this. You have two friends, both of whom are dear to you. You have had a close relationship with them in the past. But now, every time you visit, they argue together. They pay no attention to your presence in their home. You can barely get a word in edgewise in the conversation. And when you get the attention of one of your friends, everything that friend talks about is filled with the disturbance of the relationship with the other. They end up throwing things at each other, and finally you decide it is time for you to go.

This is what it is like for the sacred in the human experience. It comes to visit our consciousness. But the two friends—thought and feeling—are squabbling. Disturbed feelings demand the attention of the person's thoughts. Thoughts are under constant barrage from disturbed feelings, which are usually ignored until they become so overwhelming that they dominate the awareness. Or the person ends up thinking about what could be done to make the feelings happy. That usually involves doing something physically.

More of what is thought to make the feelings happy—more money, more food, more friends, more sex, and more drugs. And less of what is not making the feelings happy, which is mostly the result of more money, more food, more friends, more sex, and more drugs. Meanwhile, the sacred is ignored and the person cannot understand why there is a hollow and empty feeling inside. And sometimes, without correcting what is happening between their thoughts and their feelings, they attempt to have a spiritual experience. But the sacred has long ago left the house.

This is the unhappy drama that is occurring within so many people. It is a dynamic between mind and emotions that blocks the spiritual from entering the world. Because it is happening within people, it is replicated among people. Men and women often play out this drama between themselves, with a woman demanding that a man make her happy, and a man vacillating between ignoring those demands and making vain attempts to satisfy them.

This pattern of replication between the internal dynamic and the relationship drama also works in reverse. Because, in fact, we learn this fractured pattern by observing it in personal relationships—first of all, between parents and other adults when we are a child. We then replicate within us what we see in the dynamic that goes on outside us.

The pattern is broken when thought and feeling both enter deeply into the sacred; when they open to it in profound ways and cherish the experience together, sacred thought feeding sacred feeling and sacred feeling inspiring sacred thought. Now the veil that has been present in consciousness is turning transparent.

A spiritually asleep person is satisfied with an opaque veil—a state of awareness in which there is little consciousness of the sacred. So many who consider themselves spiritually aware settle on a translucent veil—like a window made of frosted glass. They have enough conscious awareness to let some sunlight come through from the other side of the window. But the shape and pattern of that reality is only a blur, so it ends up having little immediate relevance to how they live their life. They are interested in letting more light come through. Nonetheless, they are still committed to a manipulation of the physical world as their best effort to relieve their emotional disturbance. So they are not interested in living a life that is guided by what is on the other side of the glass. The sad truth is that they do not want to know what is there.

With compassion, you can see that people are struggling with this. And unless you are really different from almost everyone else on the planet, you have struggled with these issues in the past. Today, you can practice thoughts that contemplate, with compassion, how you are feeling, and give your feelings the gift of thoughts filled with what is sacred to you. You can let your feelings go as deeply as they want, to an experience of the sacred, so that they inspire your thinking with that experience. As you make space for this—a time and a place set aside to let it happen—you will find that the power and light of the sacred warms your body and empowers you to serve the sacred in your life. You find that the sacred has never left you and it never will. The window in your consciousness has turned transparent and is now there as a golden, sacred veil that is with you always.

As a sun builder, this sacred veil is a profound tool in your work. With clear thoughts and feelings, the warmth and the light of the sun can shine through you into the creative field inhabited by the people in your life. This allows the great gift you have to offer to the world to be given. It demonstrates to others what it is like to have thought and feeling in love with the sacred, in concert with one another. You have now become a priest or a priestess of the sacred veil.

Where in your life are you spiritually asleep?
What is it that you don't want to see or acknowledge?
What can you do to allow the presence of the sacred to be
fully infused into your life?

Your Presence

I dare not look over my shoulder
to look for your presence
as I know you are there
and could not stand to doubt
or be seen looking.

Yet as I come and go
You hover there as
a firefly in my thoughts,
the shade of oaks in summer,
the power of a thunderstorm rolling across the plains.

This feast is for you.
This day, this hour,
this glory ascends to you
in hallowed flame.

The Cross of Life

One of the most ancient symbols of what it is to be a human being is the cross of life. It appears in many forms throughout ancient cultures, long before Christianity. Over a century ago, English author John Denham Parsons wrote about the significance of the cross in a book titled *The Non-Christian Cross:*

> *The figure of the cross is the simplest possible representation of that union of two bodies or two sexes or two powers or two principles, which alone produces life.*
>
> *For the ancients cannot fail to have perceived that all life more immediately proceeds from the union of two principles; and the first, readiest, simplest, and most natural symbol of Life, was consequently one straight line superimposed upon another at such an angle that both could be seen; in other words, a cross of some description or other* (page 59).

So in its simplest of forms, the cross is a horizontal line symbolizing our human capacity that exists in the world of space and time, intersected by a vertical line representing the animating power of the universal that gives us life. Here is a Celtic cross that portrays this most elemental reality of our Being.

Ancient Celtic Cross
Dreamstime stock photo

Intellectual artist Leonardo da Vinci's well-known depiction of a man shows this same cross pattern as it manifests in the body, highlighting the sacred geometry of our physical proportions. How amazing that the body is a map and a living symbol for the dynamic of the cross that is so central to our Being!

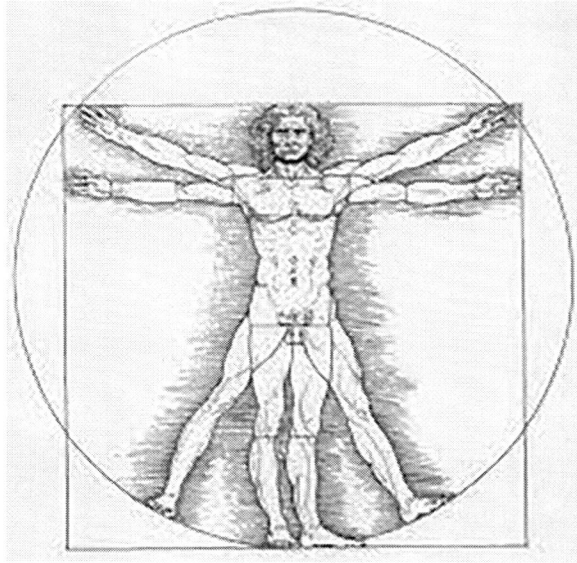

The Proportions of the Human Figure
(Vitruvian Manek), 1490 by Leonardo da Vinci
Google free image

This cross of life is evocative for us as human beings because it reveals a dynamic that is so real and so filled with great mystery. Our flesh has the power and pattern of the universe entering into it and then emanating through it into the world. The movie *Titanic* offers a contemporary depiction of this through the human body. Picture actor Kate Winslet on the prow of the ship, arms outstretched, wind blowing through her shawl and her hair. She is reveling in the living embodiment of the cross of life that we each are.

The cross of life symbolizes the spiritual at the head of the vertical beam. This is God the Possible in the heaven of our Being. In our bodies, the spiritual is located in the crown chakra, which comes to focus in the pineal gland. God the Possible crosses through God the Means, symbolized by the horizontal beam of the cross. The vertical axis is fused with the horizontal axis in our life in our heart chakra, brought to focus in the thymus gland and the physical heart.

God the Means is human consciousness—the continuum of thought and feeling. Consciousness that is open to the spiritual welcomes that reality into the physical dimension of human experience, symbolized by the foot of the vertical beam of the cross. The physical dimension is God the Manifest.

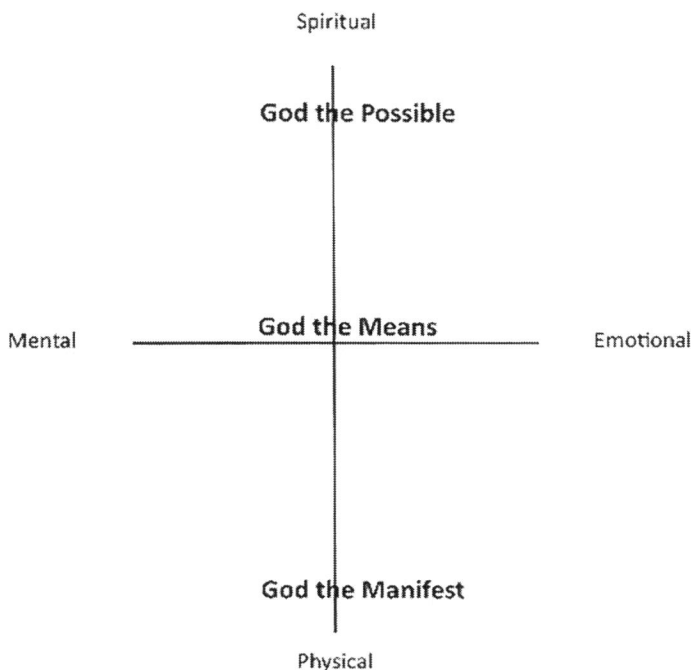

Spiritual

God the Possible

Mental   **God the Means**   Emotional

God the Manifest

Physical

How simple! How basic! Our human flesh has this intersection with the cosmic energy within it. As consciousness opens, we are fusing with the cosmic energy within all the atoms of our body. The energy we receive is cosmic in nature because it is, ultimately, the same power that pervades all of Creation, from the atom to the stars.

That power manifests differently, depending on the scale and the form through which it appears. It manifests in a unique way in us as human beings, and there is a unique way we receive it. Even though at a lower scale of creation within us—at the level of the atoms of our body—the power of creation manifests the same way it does at an atomic level throughout Creation.

At the level of the whole human being, the power of creation depends on the nature of human thought and emotion. It depends on consciousness to get fully through to us. That is why the energy field working in your body shifts and changes as you think different thoughts. The same happens for anyone. The quality of thought evokes an emotional pattern that, in turn, creates changes in the physical body and in the energy pattern of the person.

Any true spiritual practice assists a person to engage consciously in this process. When our thoughts turn to the sacred nature of the power and pattern of the spiritual, our feelings become involved too, and our feelings begin to open. There is a different sensation in the body. The body is being bathed in positive thought and feeling and in the energy that is then released through it.

When the cross is activated in you, you live in the confidence that the possibility that you perceive can manifest in your life. It is manifesting in your life, even now. You are living your dream in so many ways. For this to become real for you, you have to face all the levels of disbelief that are present in consciousness. Some people say they believe in God, by whatever name. But whether or not they do, most people believe so much more strongly in the impossibility that anything wondrous could happen in their life. Their god is the impossible, not God the Possible.

Your thoughts and feelings are the means by which God the Possible manifests in your life. This is the area in which you can make a conscious choice to open to the possible and then feel that possibility, whatever it is, deeply. As you drink in those thoughts and feelings, you are playing your role as God the Means. And then, as you act on these thoughts and feelings in the world—as you express them and give them form—you are letting God the Manifest appear. Your actions in the world are now filled from within with the power of God the Possible, with you as God the Means. You are bringing the fusion of energy and form.

The ancients depicted the cross within a sun. In cultures around the world, east and west, north and south, this symbol has appeared over millennia. This photo is of an ancient sun cross of stone in Estonia.

Sun cross in village Ervita, Estonia
Photo by Romeo Koitmäe via Wikimedia Commons

These images are ancient crosses from 4000 to 1000 BC. Many of them are sun crosses.

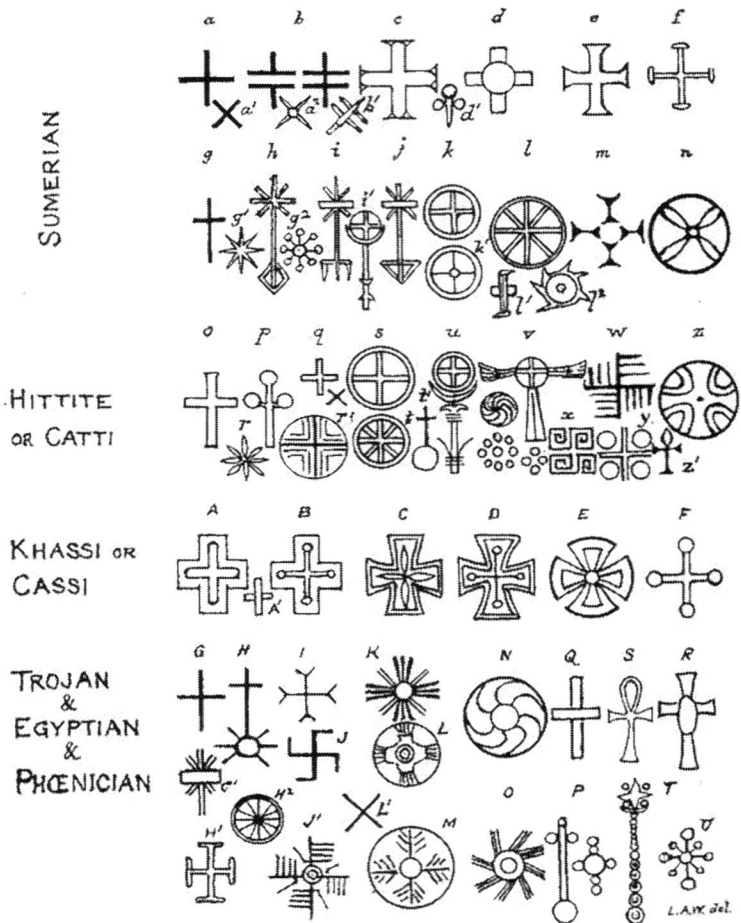

FIG. 46.—Sun Crosses, Hitto-Sumerian, Phœnician, Kassi and Trojan, plain, rayed, and decorated on seals, amulets, etc., 4000–1000 B.C.

NOTE.—Compare with Ancient Briton forms in Fig. 47; and note, re "Celtic" Cross, numbers i¹, k to n and r¹ to v and z. Detailed references in footnote on p. 296.

Image from http://www.jrbooksonline.com/pob/pob_ch20.html

As your thoughts and feelings open to God the Possible . . .

As you are God the Means, the instrument for what is possible in your creative field to become God the Manifest . . .

As you are a living cross . . .

Your human form is becoming a radiant instrument of warmth, light, and gravity, manifesting in your world. You are becoming a sun.

What is one way that you can embrace God the Possible?
What comes to mind? How does it make you feel?

This Day

This day the heavens open
And a new sun breaks forth,
From shore to shore
And from sea to shining sea.
This day we gaze across the skies
To see each other clad in golden rays of morning
With smiles of fulfillment,
Quickened by the salt spray
Rising from the granite cliffs
At the shores of our blue green home.

In the sight of stars and planets,
Arcturus and his sons,
Galaxies watch this day of celebration,
They laugh with stellar joy
To see us here now,
Face to face
In love,
In wonder,
Re-creating this precious planet
In our image

Even as we are re-created in thine,

O Lord most high,

Prince of peace

And the very soul of love.

I Am Building a Sun

There is an inner voice of truth calling. It inspires honesty and clarity in the way we relate to our own life and to other people. If we are to hear the voice that speaks with us and be that voice in our world, it takes a steady listening and our willingness to let the expression of that inner voice of truth come all the way through. And a person has to let any internal mental noise recede so that the voice may be heard.

Accord. Peace. Serenity. Letting those qualities reign internally, a person's inner voice can take root and grow in the realm of their thoughts and feelings. A person can find that what is happening in them is like the rising of the sun. There is an inner radiance that sheds light on a person's experience and on their world. All of the human capacity is activated and inspired by the rising of the sun inside them. And the internal friction that arises in this process—the resistance of heart and mind—is called to harmony through the rising of the sun. Internal friction is transformed to fusion.

The voice that speaks with you is calling you to be a sun. It is building a sun in you and, as it does, you are building a sun with other people. Your internal radiance is bringing you into creative relationship with others who are having that same experience.

Accord. Peace. Serenity. These qualities that let a sun be built in you allow a sun to be built among you and other people. As you bring these qualities to your relationships with other people, you turn any friction that appears between you and another person to fusion. You have the pleasure and fulfillment of being part of a collective sun. The warmth and the light of the sun are now coming through us together. The gravity of the sun is working in our world, drawing people toward the source of their own radiance—to their own experience of being a sun in their world.

What might be at risk for you to be a sun? If you are a sun today, you might have to be a sun tomorrow, and you might not feel like it. You might put yourself on the spot. You might have to take a stand in your life. You might become subject to ridicule. It might be hard to be a sun. You might lose who you thought you were.

There are many reasons that people avoid their opportunity to be a sun and their opportunity to build a sun with others. It can seem safer and easier to maintain a state of friction inside oneself and with other people. It can seem to be risky to let the internal friction be transformed to fusion. It can seem even riskier to let the friction with others be transformed to fusion. But of all the risks that people face in their life, there is none greater than the risk that they would miss their opportunity to be a sun and to build a sun with other people.

Here are five statements from the perspective of being a sun.

I am expanding the borders of my tent.

I am expanding what I include in my world. I am expanding what I am willing to touch. The world of what I love and include and bless is growing. I am expanding the borders of my tent.

I am extending my vibration into new territory.

The energy that moves through me is touching people and places that it has not touched before. There is a creative influence emanating from me that is bringing a new opportunity to people's awareness. I am extending my vibration into new territory.

I am moving the hearts of people as they have never been moved before.

The voice that speaks in and through me brings blessing that transforms emotion. What seemed heavy becomes light. What seemed unbearable is now part of life. I am inspiring the great desire to let the radiance of the sun flood through. I am moving hearts of people as they have never been moved before.

I am building a sun.

I am calling to my world and the people in it to join together in accord, to be a sun in living expression. To collectively provide the substance of consciousness that allows the light of the sun to be comprehended and available to people everywhere. I am building a sun.

I am bringing what is mine to me.

There are circumstances, there is physical substance, and there are people who are meant to be part of a sun. There are people on earth today who are destined to be with me and do this with me. And I am bringing them to me, because I am building a sun.

These are the words of the voice that speaks with me. They are words of a sun builder.

I am expanding the borders of my tent.

I am extending my vibration into new territory.

I am moving the hearts of people as they have never been moved before.

I am building a sun.

I am bringing what is mine to me.

Are these your words too?

We are expanding the borders of our tent. It is ultimately one voice and one tent. That tent is not an organization. That tent includes all people everywhere who hear the voice of truth that speaks with them. All such people are brothers and sisters. All are welcome in this tent.

It simply requires openness, yielding, and surrender to hear the voice that speaks with us, to listen unwaveringly and then give it steady expression in our living. With accord, peace, and serenity, we can find a new level of honesty with other people so that we can say what is so.

We can speak about everything we need to speak about together, because there is the surround of the sun that holds it all. The radiance of the sun turns friction to fusion, and our fusion brings the radiant release of the power of love, the power of the sun.

Say these words (or those of your own choosing that allows you to radiate the power of love, the power of your sun).

I am expanding the borders of my tent.

I am extending my vibration into new territory.

I am moving the hearts of people as they have never been moved before.

I am building a sun.

I am bringing what is mine to me.

Do this practice for a week, at least once a day.

What are you noticing about how you feel?

What are you noticing about what's happening in your world?

Your Sovereignty

The story of King Arthur drawing the sword, Excalibur, from a block of marble stone rings through time, inspiring people to this day. Whatever the real history of Arthur, Merlin, and the Round Table might have been, this story of how he came to be king is rich with sacred symbolism. It is the story of how anyone may claim their own sovereignty.

As the story goes, Arthur was the son of the former king, Uther Pendragon. Arthur was hidden away at birth by Merlin in a time of chaos in the kingdom, for fear of his life.

Is this not how it is for most people? By nature, they have qualities of a king or queen. It is their birthright. They are noble, even regal, but they live in a chaotic world that seems to be a threat to their nobility, as if they could not dare to expose their true identity to others. They have the capability to bring peace and order to their world and to let it prosper. But that capacity is not only hidden to the world, it is hidden to themselves. And for it to be inherited, the capacity to carry the sovereignty that is the person's birthright has to be developed.

When Arthur came of age, Merlin set the sword, Excalibur, in an anvil on a marble stone, with the following inscription:

Whoso pulleth out this sword of this stone and anvil is
rightwise king born of all England.
~ Sir Thomas Malory, *King Arthur and His Knights* ~

Howard Pyle illustration from the 1903 book
Public domain

As this transpires, Arthur is the squire to his adopted brother, Sir Kay. When Sir Kay forgets to bring his sword to a tournament, he asks Arthur to fetch it for him. Being locked out of the house, Arthur resorts to stealing into the churchyard alone and drawing the sword from the stone and anvil for Sir Kay. Sir Kay attempts to claim the kingship for himself, but it is only Arthur who is able to draw the sword and put it back again, and thus Arthur is crowned king.

Arthur represents that guileless reality within all people, who has no designs to be sovereign—no need for worldly position. Arthur's motive is to be of service to his brother. That desire to be of service is the beginning of a journey in life that takes people to their own sovereignty. It is not the ambitious Sir Kay who ascends the throne, nor the bickering lords of the realm. It is the guileless Arthur who, at first, draws the sword from the stone with no audience and no fanfare.

The sword is found in a block of cold marble, sitting in the churchyard at Christmastime. What is that cold marble from which anyone has to claim their sovereignty? It is the stony human heart, without compassion and frozen by fear. Like Sir Kay, a person may aspire to greatness, as they think of it. They may sense that they have something significant to accomplish in their life. But as long as their emotions are like that cold block of marble, they can only pretend to be who they know they really are. Only the compassion that inspires us to serve can melt the stony heart and transform it, so that it gives us our sovereign power. Only the melted human heart gives us the virility and the fertility to truly serve our world and the people in it.

There are many forms of fear. There is *acrophobia*, the fear of heights; and *arachnophobia*, the fear of spiders. There is *ablutophobia*, the fear of washing. The greatest of all fears is fear of the sovereignty within. *Adonai* is a Hebrew name for sovereignty, so this fear is *adonaphobia*, fear of sovereignty.

A true sovereign—someone who offers real service to their world—brings both love and truth to the realm. Most people are afraid of them both. Love is what makes all people and all of Creation the same. We are part of one reality, animated by one universal power. There is a deep-seated fear in people of the oneness of all Being. There is a fear that we would lose ourselves; that we could lose our uniqueness and what makes us different; we would lose the ability to carve out our own path and our life. There is a fear that we could be cheated by love and that the universe might not really care about us in the end. What looks like love could turn out to be a malevolent force that works for our demise, not our blessing.

Truth is what makes us all different. The universe has order to it; so while we are all animated by the same universal power, we are all different. No two people are just the same, and we each have our own unique place in the world. The fear is that the differentiating power of the universe could give us a place that is not the one we want—at the bottom of the organization chart, in a lower tier of society, or the black sheep of the family. Or when talents and abilities are passed out, we drew the short straw. If we submit to the ordering power of the universe, we could end up having to do something we do not want to do.

So often people find themselves fending off love, however it might come to them, from within and from without. And then they try to establish their own self-determined way of being different. In the process, a person can experience themselves as separate from the sovereign power within them and be afraid of it. Fear grips the person's heart, and they have the ongoing experience of feeling impaled emotionally, just as the cold marble is impaled by the sword.

Adonaphobia shows up as fear of authority. In the world the way it currently is, there is good reason for people to be afraid of authority. Yet still, the path to personal freedom compels a person to rise above that fear so that they own their authority, their authorship for their life. *Adonaphobia* also shows up as unresolved issues with parents. Those issues can be crippling for people, sometimes even into their senior years.

Turning back to the King Arthur story, the anvil represents the means by which *adonaphobia* may be transformed. It is interesting that while T. H. White's 1938 novel was titled *The Sword in the Stone,* the original Thomas Malory 15th-century text makes it clear that there was an anvil on top of the stone, and the sword was drawn from them both. An anvil is used by a blacksmith to make a sword. There has to be an application of heat to the steel, and then a pounding on the anvil. Both are needed. Pounding cold steel will not create a sword.

The heat and the pounding represented by the anvil are the living of a life of service that transforms a person. It is the process by which the heart melts and gives a person sovereignty. Without the fire of love welcomed into the heart, a person is just pounded by the circumstances of life. They are beaten down over time. When the fire of love is present, the substance of the heart becomes malleable. The emotional body is shaped and formed so that it becomes an expression of the sovereign power and authority, which the person had feared. The person's sovereignty becomes available to bring vitality, fertility, order, and love to the world.

Here is the telling of that experience in the story:

Thereupon Arthur went to the cube of marble stone and he laid his hands upon the haft of the sword that was thrust into the anvil. And he bent his body and drew very strongly and, lo! the sword came forth with great ease and very smoothly. And when he had got the sword into his hands, he swung it about his head so that it flashed like lightning.

~ Howard Pyle, The Story of King Arthur and His Knights ~

Picture yourself, man or woman, as a young sovereign, like Arthur, pulling your sword from what has been cold, hard stone. Picture yourself raising it high above your head so that it flashes like lightning. Feel the honor and dignity of your nobility coming into your body. Know what that nobility is saying about who you are and what you have come to do in your realm.

I retold this story of Arthur in South Africa in the presence of a Zulu woman who has become a friend. She is a great teacher and a visionary leader. Her grandmother was a *sangoma*, a medicine woman, and she knew that the mantle of her grandmother had been passed to her. But in ways that only she fully understands, she had left that legacy behind in her village as she became a strong voice for the building of a new Africa.

Arthur's story spoke to her across time, across culture and race, and across gender. It reminded her of the sacred cloth she had left in a chest in her village, and how it was a symbol of a piece of her birthright, her legacy, and her destiny, that she had left behind. In those moments, she committed to retrieve that sacred cloth and her birthright from her village. And, in so doing, to find healing in her heart and a new beginning for her life.

So let your heart be fused with the fire of love and transformed by a life of service; claim your sovereignty from out of whatever stoniness there is of your own emotional body. You will inherit what has been rightly yours all along—the nobility that is your birthright and the capacity to lead with wisdom and compassion. You will carry to your world the opportunity for peace and order and abundant life.

Are you allowing your fear of sovereignty and the fear of your own authority to prevent you from fully stepping into your birthright, your legacy, your destiny? What would it mean for you to fully own your birthright as a sovereign?

For All the Sons and Daughters

I want to wrap this world in a poem
for all the sons and daughters
who walk this earth
looking for the way home.

And in it I place treasures of the earth,
like the Concord grapes
on the banks of the Saugatuck,
and the sun as it rose
over the hills of Jordan.

And next to these things
will be the sweetest love,
fairy dust on a young boy's pillow
that fills his head
as his growing strength
fills his bones and biceps;
and dreams of motherhood
that flow like mountain streams
through the flesh of a young girl.

For all those sons and daughters,

this poem will tell a story

as it never has been told,

of courage and vision

and of the strength of ordinary people

who have touched something great;

a story of how they carried through

no matter what,

and how life is like that

if you want to know the gold at its core,

that victory that you have

when you have given all,

and having given it,

know you belong to the One you serve,

and then to those dear ones

who walk this life with you.

I Prevail

There is a great tendency in our culture to attribute the cause of things to the world of space and time. It seems easier to believe that the causative factors in our life are things that happen away from us, as opposed to inside us, and in the past as opposed to the present. The Big Bang Theory is one example of this. It pushes the causative factor for creation as far as it could possibly get from the individual.

Another example comes from the medical world, where science traces the cause of health, and the lack of it, to all kinds of physical factors— nutrition, exercise, and the sun, to name a few.

When I was taking a university biology course, a professor explained how the human body works. He carefully described how one thing causes another. He traced it back to the ribonucleic acid (RNA) and the deoxyribonucleic acid (DNA) of the cell. Finally, the chain of events traced back to an event that cannot be explained. It seems that the nucleus of the cell simply decides to act. Isn't that how it is with effects that are traceable to a cause in space and time? You can track it back so far, but you never reach the true point of origin, on that basis. What made the Big Bang bang? What told the DNA to give the message to the cell to divide?

In facing these things, we come face-to-face with the reality that the universe is vibrating from the inside. Everything is moving to an invisible rhythm. We are aware of our movements as human beings around the planet. It can tend to look like we, and a few of the other forms of nature, are the only things moving, while everything else is standing still.

The rocks seem to be standing still; the trees seem to be more or less standing still. For many people, they are far away enough from the animal kingdom that they are largely unaware of all the movement that is happening in it. Of course, if you had time-lapse photography, you would notice that our whole world is moving, and so is the rest of the universe.

There is a vibration coming from inside all things, and there is a rhythm to it. The human rhythm can be out of sync with the vibration emanating from within the human experience. If that happens to a car, or some other mechanical device—if a moving part is out of sync and starts to vibrate in a way that it is not supposed to—metal fatigue can set in. Some part of the car can break. Is a human being that different? Conscious attunement brings the rhythm and a vibration that is natural and right for each person. Thought and feeling play a critical role in that attunement.

We have been taking note of Japanese author Masaru Emoto's research on water. We are about 70 percent water, so it seems to be an important topic. Emoto found that thoughts and words have an impact on water. He took photographs of the molecular structure of water and what happens to it when people are thinking and saying different things. For instance, when the name "Adolph Hitler" was taped to a bottle of distilled water, there was a negative change in the molecular structure. When the words "Thank you" were taped to a bottle of water, there was something beautiful that happened in the crystalline structure of the water.

From Emoto's experiments, we know that there is something that we do consciously with our thoughts that impacts our physicality. But we are made of more than just water. We have a physical body, but we each have an emotional body as well. Our emotional body is, in many ways, watery, and it is connected to what is happening in the fluids of our body. So the mental attitudes we hold and the words that we speak have an impact on our waters and on our emotional body.

A creative mental attitude opens us up to our natural vibration and rhythm. It invites that power emanating from deep inside us to move in our experience. Do you think that power might have an impact on our emotional realm? There are mental attitudes that have a negative impact. For instance, if we are constantly agonizing over what has happened in the past, it is hard for the creative vibration of life to come through.

The body is involved in all this too. Feelings that resonate with our own creative vibration help bring physical health. There are many fluids in the body that, at the physical level, provide some control. For instance, the hormones from our endocrine glands provide balance for what is happening physically. Our thoughts have something to do with those hormones. And when those glands are operating in balance, there's a balance kept in the body, and we become strong and capable of bringing the vibration of who we are into the world.

The biblical story of the First Day of Creation is relevant to this consideration. "And the Spirit of God moved upon the face of the waters" (Genesis 1:2, KJB). Whoever originally wrote those words didn't have the advantage of Dr. Emoto's research. But in their own terms, they were saying that in the beginning of all Creation and in the beginning of our own creating, the vibration of what comes from an invisible reality moves on the face of the waters.

The face of the waters is the surface. But the literal meaning of the word *face* suggests something else. When you see someone's face, you see their conscious awareness through their eyes and their smile. So the face of our waters is the conscious part of our awareness that is on the surface. The spirit of God moves on that.

This story of Creation suggests that there is something we do consciously that relates to our whole feeling body. That conscious action is *critical* for the vibration of who we are to move through our whole capacity. It is where we have the choice to assume an attitude that will either empower or disable us. The healthy function of our emotional nature depends on whether we allow the *face* of our waters to be open to the creative movement of the vibration originating within us. It depends on our creative mental attitude.

Creative mental attitude is also critical for our thinking. Do you think well when you are depressed or in deep grief or when you are afraid? Psychologists call the emotion of shame "a global assault on the self." They have discovered that if shame is filling a person's capacity, a large part of the person's function shuts down. If people experience overwhelming shame, their thinking shuts down, their feelings shut down, and their decision-making process shuts down.

Of course, most people don't walk around paralyzed in that way. But how many people experience diminished personal capacity due to shame? How else might you explain the diminished capacity for thought that we sometimes notice? We do become stupid when we act out of an emotional body that has flared up, when we act out of what Eckhart Tolle calls "the emotional pain body." At the root, all emotional pain is shame.

We can do something about our own emotional body because our emotional body has a face—it has a conscious component. We probably don't understand everything that is going on in our own emotional body, but there are things that we are conscious about. There is the power of consciousness and, with that, the power of choice. We can choose to open up to the power of who we are.

We find that there are already structures in the feeling realm, just as there are structures in the water of Emoto's experiments. Where do they come from? From a space and time perspective, they come out of our past—perhaps from our parents, our upbringing, school, or culture. Wherever they come from, there are structures already in our water—our patterns of feeling that create patterns of acting. For many people, they simply decide to move from structure to structure, moving from one mood to another, never really becoming conscious, never owning the fact that there is a face to those waters—that they have a choice and that there is a vibration that they could bring into those waters that would change it, that would make it different.

If you meet somebody like that, they are probably in some trouble, and you are probably going to look for a way to say to them, "It could be different. You don't have to go from emotional state to emotional state. You could open up to another possibility. You could bring the creative power of who you are into your feeling realm, and it *would* look different."

There is a way you are meant to function, so that your conscious mind is playing its role in opening up to the vibration of what's emanating from your core—in opening up to the true cause for all creation, including your own life. This is what opens you to experience fusion with the spiritual aspect of your Being. Knowing that fusion, you are bringing the power of fusion to your world.

So here is a creative mental attitude that can open us up to the vibration of invisible cause, "I prevail." Whether the fulfillment of that is today or tomorrow, this year, next year, next decade, next lifetime, *I prevail.* I prevail in *all* things. Who I am prevails, and who you are prevails, in all things.

I am a Creator Being who prevails always and in all things. And I and we have created time and space just to give it a chance to all work out. But I prevail. Living in that reality, the patterns that naturally form out of the invisible take form.

Are there self-shaming messages in your thoughts that are imprinting on your emotional body? Try adopting a truthful, positive message.
See if that doesn't transform friction to fusion.

Yes to the New World

I am that force and power
That lifts a man
From his lowest hour;
From that time in his life
When he stares at
What will not be,
And what cannot happen.

I am that inner urge
That defies the dead,
The locked up,
The pathetic round
Of the impossible,
And like the earth's
Tectonic power,
Shakes and reforms the
Solid to dust
And back again
And says no to what will end
And yes to the new world that awaits.

One Beast, One Angel

The human experience is transformed through prayer. Your life, your family, your world—your prayer changes it all. We have that power, each of us, if we will avail ourselves of it.

Prayer is expressed openness to the spiritual. It is God the Means opening to God the Possible. It is the deliberate opening of the dual channels of thought and feeling to the potential for your creative field.

As consciousness opens to the spiritual, prayer is also the creative expression of God the Possible through God the Means. It is high vibration resonating through human thought and feeling, and then spoken and acted on in the world. It is God the Possible *entering* the world through the dual channels of thought and feeling, and creating God the Manifest in the human experience. It is the spiritual moving through consciousness into the physical.

The prayer that transforms human consciousness is not a hope that God will do something about what we think is wrong. It is not a stale religious utterance. True prayer magnifies the awareness of what is whole—the wholeness of a person and the wholeness of all living things. It invokes the implicate order of being in consciousness.

Generally speaking, people think of their own conscious awareness as belonging to themselves personally and individually. But the fact is that the consciousness of humanity is not just seven billion fragments. It is one field of consciousness. The individual is a focalization of consciousness inside the larger body of humanity. So when we are praying over what is present in our awareness, we cannot help but speak into the whole body of consciousness to which we are connected—ultimately all of humanity.

When the power of prayer is activated through you, there are people who are drawn at many levels. They may be drawn to be physically close to you. Their thoughts may be drawn in the direction of your thinking; their feelings may resonate with yours. Their spirit may join with yours, even though they have never met you or even heard of you. When the power of prayer is at work through you, you are attracting to yourself those people who are drawn to join you in your prayer.

This world needs the power of prayer in human consciousness. Why? Because there is something in the nature of human beings that is a beast. We can see the beastliness at large in the world. There is a quality of human character that seems to be bent on destruction, both self-destruction and the destruction of others. And that same beastly aspect of human nature is causing the destruction of life on Planet Earth. Bound in an unending cycle of reaction to what seems to be wrong in the world, the beast in people sows seeds of destruction. Then the results of that sowing bring even more fear and more reaction; more friction between us and a world from which we are becoming increasingly alienated.

The beast I am talking about is not any power or influence external to humanity. It is no external devil or alien influence. It is simply the thought and feeling of human beings that are focused on the physical, without openness to God the Possible, and entrained with the thoughts and feelings of other human beings who are focused on the same thing.

So invoke the power of prayer to transform all human consciousness, beginning with your own. It is the power of the vibration that is sourced in the reality that there is one Sovereign Being, one Universal Being, whose consciousness this is.

Here are words of Sovereign Being that bring the vibration of prayer to the creative field.

This is my consciousness, for my use. I am sovereign in this realm.
These are my feelings, my thoughts. This is my life. I created it. I have
power over it because it is mine. And this human nature that has
been a beast, a beast that eats a person up inside, is mine, for my use.
And the power that I have ascribed to this beastly nature is my power.
It is my power of love, which is the power behind all Creation.

If you experience a loss of inspiration, a loss of energy, a loss of personal power in your life, here is something to ponder:

There is plenty of power for all of us. But what is that power being used for? If we are giving our power to the beast in us, it eats us up. We are here to own the beast, to realize that any power the beast has is my power, for my accomplishment in the world, for my achievement, for my transformation. This is my transforming power that I bring to the people and to the world around me. This power is for creation. There is plenty of power, plenty of life. There is plenty of love. It is all mine, for my use.

But this isn't just an individual matter. We bring together one focalization of consciousness in the body of humanity, and we are not alone. There is a folk anthem I learned from Andrew and Lyell Horwood, dear friends in South Australia. The song says it so well, "We are one, but we are many."

These words appear on the Great Seal of the United States: E Pluribus Unum—out of the many, one. Or perhaps it should be the other way around, "Out of the one, many." There is both plurality and unity in the body of humanity. Those who read the words of this book are many—but they are also one.

For an individual who is experiencing isolation, this is what that looks like: "I am experiencing this all by myself and I am all alone in it. And it's really different from what everybody else is experiencing."

Anybody who has done some serious work in themselves and with other people finds out that this just isn't so. The human experience runs in repetitive patterns. They replicate throughout humanity. So even if people are feeling isolated, they are feeling isolated together with many other people who are feeling isolated, wherever they might be around the globe.

When the beast rises up in people, they tend to think that this is all about them and their own unique experience—their challenges, their limitations, their past, and their shame. Or if it rises up in somebody else, it's all about that person—he or she is the beast!

The truth is there is one beast, even though it manifests through many human beings around the globe. And using the word *angel* to refer to the sovereign reality of the Being that you are and that I am, there is one angel. There are many angels, but there is one angel.

We can speak for the angel that we are individually, but the game of life we are playing as human beings is not just individual. It often seems to be. It does come to focus in you and it comes to focus in me. So that is true. It might seem as though you are all alone in confronting the beast in your life. But there is one beast. It is not just your beast; it is the *beast*. And it isn't just you confronting it. The angel faces the beast. The one angel has already confronted the one beast. The angel created the human capacity that has taken on beastly attributes.

It serves the purposes of the beast for you to think it is just your little individual beast or that it is just a beast in someone else; because when you really know that all around the world there is one beast and one angel, for you, the contest is over. Until that point, it might seem like there is a contest. It might seem like you are wrestling with whatever it is in yourself or in other people, and the friction might seem to go on and on. When you see that there is one beast and one angel, it is over. You are welcoming fusion in your life.

At that point, you can hear and speak the voice of the angel that says, "This body of humanity is mine, and everything about it is mine, for *my* expression, for the fulfillment of my purposes on the earth, to bring *my* spirit. This body is here to bring the vibration of cosmic love. This body is mine. And because it is mine, I do not have to fight with it. I possess it. It becomes fused with who I am." Where there are people who see this and know it, the contest is over.

Can anything stop the vibration of love? I do not care what wall a person puts up, it cannot stop love. And the beast in you can erect no wall that would stop the vibration of love. The angel does not contend with the wall. To the angel, the wall is as nothing.

You have the opportunity on this day to change the way you are playing the game of life, to change the rules by which you are playing and bring what is the ultimate game changer: the knowledge that there is one beast and there is one angel, and what has seemed to be a beast is your capacity on earth for your expression, to bring your power, your authority, your love, and your truth into the world.

Cliff Barry, the founder of Shadow Work® seminars, says that the elders in the circle have to disbelieve. In other words, if a group is to thrive, there have to be leaders who choose not to buy into any negative thought pattern that would sabotage the group. They have to disbelieve that the beast has any power other than the power you give it.

The creative field we share as human beings is a field for transformation because there are elders here; elders who hold this field and create a context where other people can awaken to who they are, so that people around the world can find that their thoughts and feelings are drawn to the creative field held by the one angel. They might not know about you or about me, but they will find themselves believing that there is hope in the world, that there is something that is true and there is something that is possible, because somehow they can feel it, they can touch it themselves in our global presence, in our fusion.

All this happens because God the Means opens to God the Possible. And the one angel can speak through human consciousness to the body of humankind. To your human body. To the whole body of humankind through you.

Where can you bring the power of prayer and
the power of fusion more fully into your life?

Chapter Five

THE RAYS

OF

ENLIGHTENED THOUGHT

You cannot hate, argue, reason, fight, complain or yell at a
dark room enough to illuminate it—only by shining a light is
darkness overcome. Be that light.

~ ANONYMOUS ~

World Creates Consciousness vs. Consciousness Creates World

The truth of enlightened thinking is incredibly simple. Just as the truth of what creates unenlightened thinking is incredibly simple. They are both dynamics within a person that are dependent on the orientation of the mind.

There are religious institutions and spiritual paths that try to teach that the journey to enlightenment is long and hard. That it takes great effort and huge human discipline. It doesn't. I don't want to diminish the efforts of sincere spiritual people around the world, but I believe that any exertion of human effort or human will actually postpone enlightenment, not facilitate it.

The person who attempts to attain enlightened awareness through human effort believes that they will know it only after they expend human effort of some kind—after they fast, meditate, read, deprive themselves, exert extreme physical effort, or pray. But they don't. At least they don't have enlightened awareness unless they do what anyone could do right now—change the orientation of their mind. Because, yes, it is natural to extend effort in a human life. But that is not what creates enlightened awareness.

Consider this question regarding consciousness. Does the world around a person create consciousness? It seems logical to think that it does. When a particular event occurs, that event enters the mind through the senses. The mind then considers the event and thinks about how to make the best of it. And how to avoid all the bad things that could happen in the future.

This is thinking about the physical. You may be thinking about your own body—how it feels, what shape it is in, how you look in the mirror, how your health is, or how old you are becoming. I can guarantee you that the more you think about your body in this way, the more anxious and unhappy you will become. Unless something else enters the picture, you will become more and more worried about your body and the state it is in and what is happening to it. Anxiety and unhappiness might lead to depression and worse.

Or you may be thinking about the circumstances of your life—your job, your money, people in your life, etc. And the same is true—as long as thinking is oriented to these realities in physical form, and nothing else is entering consciousness, the mind will grow increasingly anxious and unhappy. In such a state, the world *has* created consciousness. And the results are not appealing. This dynamic leads a person to the belief and experience that they are a victim of circumstance. They have let their state of conscious experience be determined by the world, even though it does not have to be.

Try experimenting with this idea. Your consciousness could create your world. That creation will require some thinking about the physical reality around you. But more than that is required. You have to open your thoughts to the spiritual so that what is possible in the world can be conceived in your mind. The spiritual dimension of your Being is what activates the mind with new thought, new ideas, new potential, and new possibilities. It is the source of creative imagination.

Undoubtedly, you are letting this happen in some areas of your life, to whatever degree. But more and more you could live your whole life this way. You could reinvent your whole life if you wanted to—imagine how your life could potentially be and then let that vision begin to manifest.

You could encourage the people around you to have this same experience. In fact, you could welcome fresh thoughts about those people and see them with new eyes. Just by having this kind of vision of them, how they think, act, and feel could be profoundly affected. It is true that the consciousness of people around you affects the physical reality in which you live. But your consciousness might change theirs. You could be part of a global shift in consciousness that is creating a new world.

How did the world get to be the way it is now? Is it not a result of the consciousness of every person who played a part in creating it? If we could collectively create it this way, couldn't we create it a different way? And how about your individual world? Understanding that other people have played a part, haven't your own beliefs been a key factor in what has created the world of your experience? Through no fault of your own, you might have absorbed beliefs and ideas that created a reality that is less than optimal. Opening your thoughts to the unending source of light and ideas within you, those limited beliefs and ideas could change. A new world could be created from your new thought.

Take your body, for instance. You could work hard to change how you look, how your body feels, or how much you weigh. But if you have a belief, deep down in your soul, that you are not beautiful or that you are a sickly, overweight person, then all the cosmetics, all the exercise, and all the dieting might not change your experience.

So what do you believe about your body? Is it enlightened thinking? Or is it a shame-based belief, dark thinking? You might have been creating a physical reality based on your belief. And even thinking about it now could bring up more thoughts about your physicality that reinforce a sense of shame.

For instance, you might have known young women who suffer from an eating disorder. Often, they are beautiful and thin. But they can't see it and they don't believe it. The idea in their mind is stuck and they are manifesting a life based in that idea.

What is really true about your body? The truth is that your body is the temple for your incarnation. It is the temple of the living God, your temple as the angel you are. You could judge it from your human perspective. But the truth is that your body is housing the mystery of life. It is landing quantum reality through the magically creative ability of your consciousness. Think about that, not about your judgments of your body. If you allow your thoughts to orient to this reality, you will find a stream of thoughts flowing through your mind, each one revealing a deeper reality, and a deeper place within your own soul, shining light on a deeper truth. Let this stream run its natural course until it has told you all you need to know about the beauty of your incarnation and the remarkable nature of your physical body.

This is enlightened thought. It is inspired when you turn away from any preoccupation with physical reality and think about the spiritual—about the possible, about the sacred, about the essence of what you love and value. When the fire of the spiritual shines through the air of the mind, the mind can see the pattern that is emerging from the source of all Creation.

The spiritual is like lightning that illuminates the summer sky on a dark night. This is what let theoretical physicist Albert Einstein see and understand the theory of relativity, looking at a clock tower while riding on a streetcar in Bern. This is what was behind the genius of musicians John Lennon, Paul McCartney, Ludwig van Beethoven, and any truly gifted musician. This is what the Buddha experienced under the Bodhi Tree.

This diagram depicts the dynamic between the spiritual and the mental that inspires enlightened thought.

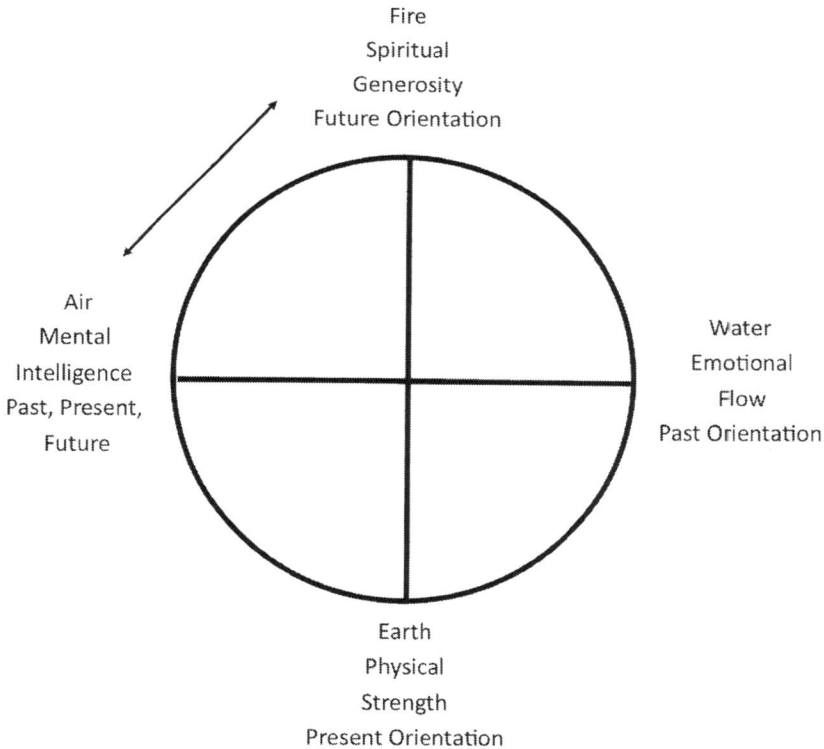

Fire
Spiritual
Generosity
Future Orientation

Air
Mental
Intelligence
Past, Present,
Future

Water
Emotional
Flow
Past Orientation

Earth
Physical
Strength
Present Orientation

We are all designed to think enlightened thoughts; to see and understand the patterns of the universe relevant to our creative field, streaming through our thinking. All it takes is a reorientation of the mind—a turning of thought to the source of all patterns and all possibility.

When has the "light come on" in your thoughts?
How could you have more of that experience in your life now?

Vessels Made New

The most incredible dance theatre piece I have ever seen was also the simplest. One of my dearest friends, Yienan Song, is a professional dancer and had invited me to one of her performances.

With her long black hair, she stood before the curtain, deep in the stage. The curtain was backlit with an azure light. Holding a huge seashell, set aflame with burning ghee and illuminating her face, Yienan walked with that seashell from the back of the stage to the front of the stage. That was it. But with such composure . . . such focus . . . with a sublime, measured, even stride. Time stood still, and we entered eternity. I cannot begin to guess for how long in earthly time.

This experience, and others like it, brought me to the realization that art can provide a window to a transcendent reality. And it is not the complexity of the art or the usual idea of human creativity that opens that window. It is the conscious intent of the artist that does it.

As a musician, I have realized that silence is precious and beautiful. It is music. And even a single tone can be magnificent, and out of it there resonates many other notes in the overtone series—less noticeable frequencies that bring harmony and character to accompany the root tone. Approached in this way, with respect for the essential elements of form, art opens windows of consciousness, most profoundly for the artist. But also for anyone who attunes to the experience that the artist has in creating the art.

But if the forms of art can be a window to a higher reality, so can the forms around us. A tree . . . a beach . . . a baby . . . even a subway ride.

During that period in our lives my wife, Joyce, and I performed and recorded with another dear friend, Michael Gaeta. We produced a CD of all-original music, *Open Green,* and the three of us composed music, together and separately. At the same time, the spiritual community in which we had been participating, Emissaries of Divine Light, was faltering. The man who had led it, Martin Cecil, had died in 1988 and much of the leadership that had been around him was leaving the organization. It was a spiritual community coming undone. For anyone who has been part of that kind of process, you know it is full of heartache and disappointment.

It was a remarkable contrast for me personally—a profound awakening to a mystical experience available within art and within all of life, and all the painful emotions of a community of people falling out of love. In the midst of this, Mike, Joyce, and I came together to create a song for solo voice and chorus, with Mike on the piano. It was June 1992 in an apartment that Joyce and I were renting in Stamford, Connecticut. We created a ritual of personal sanctification and renewal that was featured in the song, to be performed by Jeltje, a lanky, blonde Dutch woman who had been like a second mother to our daughter, Helena.

How can you describe that moment when you touch the essence of a song before it has been created? That moment is an entrance into a secret inner chamber. Within that place lies an unborn reality, and to hear it in the inner ear of heart and mind is like touching babies' flesh. It is soft and tender, sweet and precious, waiting to be born. The idea that you created it is as preposterous as the idea that you created your own child. Yes, you had a vital part to play. But it was the life source itself that created both the child and the music. As a composer, you have the supreme privilege of hearing the music and then letting it be born through you. And that is about as good as it gets.

Joyce, Mike, and I were together in this space as the song was being born. First, there was an intoxicating, evocative, chord progression that defined the verse. Then a melody that floated above the chords, as if melody and chords had barely met before. The words of the verse were instructions for the ritual:

Kneel before the altar and lift the cloth of gold,
Don your raiment, o child of the stars!
Upon your brow smear oil of olive, rich and green,
And drink the cool water placed there for your need.

Then came the chorus. It was a refrain of joy and victory. A call to enter our lives today as if for the first time:

Now has come the time of rejoicing,
Come let us worship in vessels made new!

The day came for us to perform the song at a conference at a community and conference center in New Hampshire. We drove there from New York City. As it turned out, Mike had business in New York in the middle of the conference, so he and I returned by car overnight and then drove back up to New Hampshire to perform. Six hours each way.

Whatever it takes.

We called the song "Vessels of the Temple." It was mystical. The descending minor chords and Joyce's liquid soprano singing over them drew the audience into a trance of self-renewal, while Jeltje's lithe figure glided across the stage, following the instruction for the ritual contained in the verse of the song. We shared in a healing of our spirits as Jeltje smeared the oil on her brow. Over the dark harmonies played by his left hand, Mike improvised, off-beat and evocative, jazz improvisation meeting sacred ritual.

Taking in the moment, I thought about what was happening.

We are accessing the medicine that heals our souls!

The verse gave way to the exultant major chords of the refrain. The tenors answered the rest of the chorus, "Now has come the time!" I was singing the bass part, watching Mike, ecstatic at the piano, head bobbing, rising off the bench for more leverage exercised through his long fingers as he passionately pounded out the piano part.

This is our future! Whatever is falling apart, life is grand!
Life is glorious! We are healed!

It was exultant.

Not long after that, the community and conference center in New Hampshire closed. I was given the job of selling the property with my friend, Charlene Hunter, but the grief of that experience never eclipsed the magnificence of the song. We had seen the wonder of what our lives were truly about. That has never changed for Joyce, for Mike, or for me.

That is how it is when the light of the sun shines in your awareness. When you not only see that light, but embrace it and let it shine through you. You are changed. Your life destiny is altered.

To us, the vessels of the temple were our hearts and minds and bodies. Emerging out of any sense of fear, shame and lack, our vessels are made new. Ready to receive the enlightened ideas of the universe. Ready to feel and know the possibility that the universe has in store, and ready to share it with others. Ready to let it manifest. As the final chorus of the song proclaims:

Let this company,
Let this day
Be warmed in the celebration,
Vessels made new!

Thankfully, this vision has come true in my own life and in my community, Emissaries of Divine Light. True visions always come true. Even in the midst of all that might be falling apart.

Incarnation

If you were an eternal spirit Being of the cosmos, why would you have chosen to incarnate as you? According to the Creation stories around the world, that is exactly what has happened. You've chosen to be here on this planet, in this time, and in this place. This is from a story that the Cherokee people tell:

> *In another time, the Cherokee Spirit People were in the skyvault. It was getting crowded in the skyvault, and the Great One decided it was time for spirit beings to become physical beings and spread out of the skyvault. There was a Great Council meeting of all the spirit beings to decide on the plan. The Great One said, "Those of you who choose to be a part of the creation of Mother Earth will also have to protect her. The Cherokee Spirit People have been chosen to be keepers of the secrets, and keepers of Mother Earth and all living things that go over into the physical world. They will be given the power Medicine of choice to do this."*
>
> *- Medicine of the Cherokee: The Way of Right Relationship -*

The Creation story in Genesis 1:26–27, KJB, tells a similar tale:

> *And God said, Let us make man in our image, after our likeness: and let them have dominion over the fish of the sea, and over the fowl of the air, and over the cattle, and over all the earth, and over every creeping thing that creepeth upon the earth.*
>
> *So God created man in his own image, in the image of God created he him; male and female created he them.*

The primal stories from around the world also attempt to explain how risky it is to be an eternal spirit who incarnates as a human being. Through our human experience we can lose connection, attunement, and alignment with the eternal spirit who created the human experience in the first place.

But we don't have to read myths and legends around the world to understand how problematic the human experiment can become. We know from firsthand observation and experience.

Now think about the experience from the perspective of an eternal spirit. Think of all the risks there would be for an eternal spirit to take on all the behavior patterns, all the thought processes and feelings of a human being. Think of all the bad habits, all the self-destructive tendencies, the irrationality and pettiness, the emotional rollercoaster.

To really appreciate the issue, and to let it become more specific, consider the risk of incarnating as you. Think of all your human shortcomings. Think about how you get sometimes. If you were an eternal spirit, moving freely through the cosmos, why would you take on all that?

Perhaps it seemed like it could have been fun to be in a body. But if you did decide to create a physical form into which you could incarnate, why not hardwire it to behave properly? You do have to wonder why human beings were not made more or less like a marionette, with strings pulled from the eternal without the possibility that they do not approve of the cosmic direction they are receiving through those strings. Or at least with some kind of "back door," like the computer programmers create, so that if your human capacities started to misbehave—if your thinking and feeling developed a "bug"—you could get in and fix it. Surely, if you were an eternal cosmic spirit, you could have come up with a fail-safe mechanism that would keep you, as a human being, out of all the problems you get into.

What were you thinking?

So here is the wild idea that was hatched somewhere in the eternal. Let's create a living, sentient being in whom we could incarnate. Why be just cosmic energy, when we could be human? Let's not settle for creating something so dependable and safe as a rock. Let's not settle on creating a tree, even though trees are living forms that grow and reproduce. Let's not settle on creating an animal, even though the creatures of Planet Earth are wondrous.

Let's create a being that has the capacity of choice and will—and the possibility of real calamity. Because if our incarnational facility has the capacity of choice and will, we could exercise our choice and our will in and through the incarnational facility—through the human being, as the human being. We don't want just to work *through* a physical form. We want to enter the physical form and act as it. We could be free to do as we choose on Earth. We could enter the space-time continuum, check it out, and decide what to do once we got there. Imagine that! Cosmic energy functioning through a sentient being at the physical plane. Sure it's risky. It is a high-risk, high-reward project. Let's go for it!

Does your own will ever get you into trouble?
Close your eyes for a moment and meditate on these words:
"I surrender my will as a human being to the highest reality of who I am."

Freedom for the One I Am

It is hard to imagine any form in which you could be as free as you could be through a human form. You might enjoy being another form for a while—a rock, for instance. As I look at the red sandstone cliffs where I live, they carry the story of the ages. But there are limitations in being a rock that would not be present in a human form.

How free do you think your spirit is in being you? For most people, the human experience is full of restriction. They feel the restriction and look for freedom. They feel their capacity of choice and will, and try to use it to be free. Two-year-olds are experimenting with this when they first learn to say, "No!" to their parents. Adolescents are building this capacity when they make decisions to do what they want to do, not what their elders want them to do. People in a mid-life crisis are often asserting their own choice and their own will, as distinct from the choice and will of their surrounding culture.

So what is the problem? From the human standpoint, the problem is that when people assert their own will as an individual, they don't necessarily find freedom or happiness. The experience of freedom can be elusive on this basis. But the human problem is only a reflection of the larger problem that you have as an eternal cosmic Being. You created this human capacity.

The human being was born with the potential of free will and has developed that capacity while growing up. So far, so good. But if your human capacity doesn't understand that *you* are the one who created it with free choice, so that *you* could exercise *your* will as the human being, then the capacity is off by itself, "doing its own thing," using its will to find its freedom without you. And becoming horribly unhappy in the process.

If that is what is happening, it might be time for a wake-up call— some rays of light from the sun nature of your Being. Something radical, like a personal misfortune or tragedy, might do it. Or perhaps a profound spiritual awakening. That might get the attention of your humanity. "Come back!" That might be what you, as an eternal cosmic Being, are thinking.

To be really free, the human capacity has to engage in contrarian thinking—thinking that goes in the opposite direction of what might seem logical on the face of it. Instead of thinking that you have to claim your own freedom, you have to find a way to surrender your freedom to the eternal cosmic Being who you are. Instead of being driven by your personal will, your personal choice, your personal ambition, you have to surrender your will, your choice, and your ambition to the eternal cosmic Being who you are.

If you are to free the spirit who you are, you have to accept a life of increasing restriction for your human capacities. And in accepting this restriction, the human capacities share the freedom you know as an eternal Being. This is the ultimate spiritual practice. The eternal doesn't just want to teach you and direct you from the outside, through the teaching or direction of someone else, or through a philosophy or creed. While those ways of leading might make a good start to a spiritual journey, as a destination they are the booby prize. The eternal Being who you are is not satisfied with your human compliance or obedience. It is looking for total takeover—full incarnation, full self-emergence through the human capacity. Your light is here to shine.

Think about the life of Nelson Mandela. Here is a man who was imprisoned for 27 years. He was in a situation that most would agree had great restriction. The amazing thing is that he came out the other end of that experience a free man—not only because he was released from his physical prison but also because he accepted the restriction of his situation and found that he could be free in it.

Mandela's capacity of consciousness opened to his own spirit, and in that sense his capacities became his own. So even though the cell was confining, he had his own mind and heart that became available to him. Consequently, he brought freedom and peace to his creative field. Not only was his leadership crucial in freeing South Africa from apartheid; his kindness, vision, and compassion facilitated a transition with a minimum of violence. Today, when you invoke his name in South Africa it is met with deep reverence and respect among all races. The nobility and luminous rays of his spirit have impacted the whole world.

As awfully challenging as the circumstances of his life were, he had a certain advantage over many people in this world who, even though they can move around at will, do not have their own capacity of consciousness open and available to them. Their spirit is not free in their own humanity because the capacity of consciousness is preoccupied with pursuing its own ends.

What an opportunity! Increasing restriction. But the truth is that you are set free when your human consciousness learns to accept the restriction of the circumstances as they are and, more important, to surrender to the eternal Spirit you are. Less and less freedom for your humanity. More and more freedom for you.

Where are you experiencing restriction?
How might this be freeing for you?

The Realm of Angels

What is possible for a person and what is potential in this world might seem to be a dream relating to some future time. What is possible might seem to be nonexistent, something that might take form here one day in the world as it is. But when we touch real possibility or potential, we are not just touching something that could manifest here. We are sensing an already-existing reality at another level of Being. There is an already-existing glory. There is truth and beauty before it ever manifests in a world that is perceptible by our internal intuition. This realm of potential holds the essence of what could manifest in physical form.

The realm of potential is the realm of *angels*, using that word to acknowledge that this is a range not just of energy, not just of higher consciousness, but of higher Being. And just as there is beingness in our human world, there is beingness at every level of creation. What do you think—that there is beingness here on Earth where there are people, but at higher ranges of reality, higher ranges of consciousness, there's no beingness, there is just energy and vibration? No. There are angels. There is a realm of consciousness and the work of angels. What is an already-existing reality in that realm is the potential for this realm.

What manifests in the world today is a reflection of what is in human consciousness. In many ways humanity is in the middle of a nightmare, and that nightmare is coming true. That is happening in the world at large. I hardly need to name the serious issues that are facing humanity: global warming, the risk of financial collapse, ecological devastation, to name just three.

But there are nightmares in individual lives. It manifests as addiction, mental illness, and emotional disturbance. And it's just plain unhappiness. You do not have to live long before you realize how many people are living lives of quiet desperation. It is happening in families, is it not? Behind divorce rates are agonizing human dramas between couples. Many families are holding a nightmare in consciousness and living into that nightmare, and manifesting a nightmare, in many cases.

In communities, in nations, among nations, in organizations, there is a bad dream that is manifesting in people's lives. We know that we can hold a different kind of field—a different dream and a different kind of culture that manifests a different reality.

There is the field that we share as human beings, but no matter how hard we try to make it creative, it cannot be—unless and until we realize that this field that we are holding as human beings is actually part of a larger field that is not being held by us as human beings.

There is a creative field being held by angels. There is an already-existing field that you and I did not have to invent. It does not depend or rely on us in any way. Our experience as human beings relies on what we do, but that larger creative field, that universal field, does not rely on us. It is already existing. It is being held by angels, not by us as mere human beings. It is being held by Universal Being, by the beingness of the cosmos. And when we become aware of that larger field, we become aware of possibility and potential for our field. It is the possibility and potential that what is present in that larger field could manifest on Earth.

But that only happens as we, as human beings, become aware that the purpose of our lives is to be of service to that higher and larger creative field. When we remember to shine our light . . . to be the ray of light that illuminates the path for others.

We are made to allow the pattern that is present in that field, particularly as it pertains to us, to be received, and then move through us so that pattern is manifest here, so that what is already true in potential, in the field held by angels, is now coming true in this field.

In that process, we discover that we are not just human beings, struggling to manifest something creative in our lives. We certainly are human beings—we have human capacities: mind, body, and heart. But the human capacities are here for something else. We discover that we are not only the dutiful servants of a higher reality, as human beings, but the truth of us is that we are the angel, holding a higher field.

For many people, what is real is all the trouble, all the issues, and maybe even disasters in their creative field, and then the heroic ways they are attempting to deal with those challenges. And what passes for spirituality is assistance for those heroic attempts as a human being to cope with the disasters that are being created because of a lack of awareness of this higher field.

It turns out that the field of stability, the field that is reliable and dependable and real and substantial, is not at the level where all the disasters are happening. What is truly reliable and dependable is the field held by angels. It is always there in a person's life. And what is reliable and dependable is the beingness of a person, which is your angelic nature. Through whatever issues come up, even the disasters, through whatever troubles come, that is always present. The angel is always present.

God is often looked at as being something separate, to be appealed to. Angelic reality is us, and the most stable and real and dependable thing in our life is our presence, not something other than us—because no matter what happens in your world or in mine, we can always come back to the reality of our Being, which is always present and always stable and always assured.

E pluribus unum—out of the many, one—applies not only to human beings but to angels. There are many angels and there is oneness. All the angels of heaven compose the reality of God. Just as we, as human beings, are many and we are one, so are the angels.

When there is oneness, the voice and the will of the whole can be focused by one being. And the voice of will of one being can focus the voice of being of all beings. Oftentimes grudgingly, we allow this principle to be in operation as human beings, and we allow our activities to come to focus in one place through one person, whether it is the president, the chief executive officer (CEO), a teacher, a spiritual leader of some kind, or the secretary-general of the United Nations. Begrudgingly, and suspiciously, we allow this principle to be in operation. We do not want to have anyone run away with power.

How do you think it is for the angels? The angels have an advantage when it comes to these matters. They don't have to worry about one of them becoming power hungry or going nuts. There is the wisdom of angels; there is the knowing of angels and the clarity of angels. And in that pattern it is absolutely no problem to acknowledge the oneness in the midst of the many and to allow that oneness to come to focus.

There are many aspects of individualized Being in the cosmos. Without that, it would be really boring. Contrary to what is sometimes taught in spiritual circles, it is not just a flat sea of consciousness. There are individualized aspects of Being, and there is one Being. We are one, and we are many. Human beings try to experience that together. We try to find oneness, peace, and harmony. It's oh so elusive, and impossible actually, except as the human beings involved are in total service to the already-existing pattern of oneness and harmony.

We don't have to create that. We are in that. We are that. And while we can have our checks and balances as human beings, there are no checks and balances in heaven. And while we don't want to be silly about our lives in the human world, we can live the higher awareness that we are already in love, we are already in light, we are already in harmony, we are already honoring and in service to the whole. We are already in service to the overarching pattern of Being, to the constellation of angels. I am not inviting you into a religious belief. I am inviting you to sense for yourself what is true.

Living in this awareness, we are naturally inspired. It is inspiration beyond inspiration—inspiration that knows no walls, that cannot be stopped, that just is. In being oneself and expressing the realm of the possible, there is the power of creation, the power of manifestation, and the radiance of Being that is coming through human form. But ultimately it's not coming from the human being per se. It is coming from the angel.

You might think that I am inviting you into a realm of imagination. I am inviting you to reality. What I am speaking of does not require any imagination. It requires you allowing light to be shed on what is already there but has been shrouded from your understanding until now. It requires taking some steps into the reality of Being and choosing to live from there. And I promise you, you can do that without losing touch with what it means to live a human life. In fact, by taking these steps, you will find that you are bringing the power of creation into your human life and into the creative field that surrounds you. You will not have to be keeping alive some kind of spiritual illusion, as if you're playing a game of *Dungeons and Dragons*, spiritual style.

You will be called to be more and more and more yourself, and more and more aware of what the reality of Being really is, and how it transcends your immediate human life. In fact, it transcends your whole human life and the entire creative field in which you are working as a human being. All that is being held in a far larger field, of which you are a part. You can sense that and know it and know the larger stature of your own Being, and know that in your immediate creative field there is a grand potential that is born out of the higher field.

To be about creation, you have to be undistracted from all the issues of the immediate field. Certainly, there are people and things to be cared for and new things to be created. But how is that to be accomplished if the human mind and heart manage to unplug themselves from the wisdom, power, and potential that is inherent in the field of angels?

So we have work to do. That work relates to manifestation and creation. But that part is relatively easy. The greater work that we have to do is regaining consciousness so that we are back with what is reliable and substantial. And to fully regain consciousness, and sustain conscious awareness, you will have to continually bathe your heart and mind with the light of the sun that you are. You will have to develop the habit of opening your heart and mind to the light of your Being. Then you can assist others in the process.

If you do not develop this habit, you will always be unsteady when the time comes to bring the radiance of Being and the power of creation. You will always be distracted at the hour of need, when important things in your life are coming to issue. You won't be there for someone who needs you. You won't feel the wisdom you have to meet a challenge in front of you. You won't see the golden opportunity that is staring you right in the face.

How about being present at the hour of need and through all of the creative cycle, and being so fully present that the victory in the moment is assured? If you develop a daily practice of staying spiritually conscious, then when big events arise in your life, you will be present for them—when you are meeting someone for the first time who is important to your life destiny, when your genius is needed on an important project, or when a group that you are part of needs your leadership.

And what is the victory? The victory simply is that the vision and creative power of the angel is present through a human being. You are that angel, present now through your consciousness and in your physical body. Enjoy your incarnation!

How does it feel for you when you are being fully present and aware? How could you evoke and sustain that feeling when distractions come up?

Angels in the Sleeping Darkness

The whirr of angel wings
hovers in the sleeping darkness
to surround a restless planet.

Ice flows rumble,
tsunamis tumble,
the rivers of Turtle Island
overflow their banks.
Buildings crumble,
markets stumble,
and leaders bumble,
with little oil
to fill their lamps.

And still the angel voices
whisper in the night,
to tell a different story,
filled with tales of love and glory,
and the coming of new light.

Each illumined face appears
shining from the deep,
their brilliant eyes,
like burning stars,
watch a world asleep.

As they draw near,
their voices raised,
they sing their song
of celestial praise.
"Wake up, world!
Wake up, man!
Wake up, woman!
Wake up, land!"

In far-flung places,
in open spaces
of yielded heart and mind,
like deserts winds
through canyon walls,
they speak to humankind.
Their presence felt
as much as heard,

their joy a breath away,
come listen now,
hear their song,
and all they have to say.

The Impact of Oppression on Primal Spirituality

In October 2013, I had the opportunity to lead a workshop in Stroud, England. I was teaching what I have taught for years, essentially, the subject of this book. I painted a picture of the dynamics inside a person and among people, and how they play out through the human mind and emotions. I described how changes in the way we think and feel change what manifests in our physical bodies and in the world around us. I spoke about how the symbol of the cross of life is an ancient symbol for our spirituality that predates religion.

As I spoke, people were interested and open. This was not an average group of English people. They had a particular interest in spiritual matters and in what I had to present. And still, as we lingered on the porch outside the building afterward, I reflected on what had happened. I thought about the blank looks on people's faces as I spoke about the most basic factors in human experience, about all the blank looks I have received from people over many years, and about all my efforts to understand the most elemental factors in the human experience and to share that understanding in the clearest way possible.

What is this darkness? Is something wrong with me?
Am I a confusing, inadequate teacher?

I thought about the great disbelief I have encountered when people are presented with the idea that it is not only possible but truly normal for a person to know, with assurance, the vastness of God. Or that we are capable of understanding ourselves and other people, and acting masterfully relative to our human experience.

I know from working with people at depth for many years that most people are almost deathly afraid of their own feelings. They are often plagued, almost incessantly, by their own negative self-talk—their biting criticism of themselves and other people. They often feel unsure of who or what God is, or how to live their spirituality in the world. And I have observed so many people, including so many in the generation who are now in their twenties and thirties, who feel utterly betrayed by religion and by spirituality of any kind.

I've seen the darkness of that betrayal destroy the prospect of joy and fulfillment. So the most elemental factors of what it is to be a human being so often remain a mystery for people. We say that the great existential questions are "Who am I?" and "Why am I here?" as if these were mysteries that were ultimately imponderable. But this is knowledge that is part of our primal spirituality—the innate knowing that it is natural to us when it is not smothered by cultural and religious mindsets.

As I reflected on my experience that day in Stroud, and my experiences over many years, I was left with the question: *What has happened to us that the most elemental realities of what it means to be a human being are such a mystery?*

I pictured myself as an anthropologist discovering a culture in a distant foreign land, without the light of understanding of the most essential elements of a human being. *What might I think had happened to them?* The sad answer that came flying into my thoughts was this: *These are the symptoms of an oppressed people.*

I thought about all I know about patterns of oppression and the history of Western civilization. One of the instruments of oppression is religion. Not to discount whatever virtue religion has; however, it has been used to dominate. Perhaps the most obvious form of religious oppression is persecution, such as the persecution of witches, or the persecution of Jews during the Spanish inquisition. But there are subtler forms of oppression and disempowerment carried on in the name of religion.

The Roman Empire did a masterful job of co-opting Christianity. After being instrumental in Jesus' crucifixion, they reinterpreted his message and claimed that the empire was the chief proponent of his teachings. They proceeded to co-opt the spirituality of the peoples they conquered and roll it into their new Christianity. That is why the holiday Easter is named after the Babylonian goddess of Venus, Astarte. That is why Christmas was timed to coincide with the winter solstice, even though there is no evidence that December 25 was the date that Jesus was born. And that is why the Roman Empire's church took the cross of life that was celebrated by peoples they conquered and turned it into a crucifix, a cross of death.

I thought about the dreaded symbol of Nazi Germany, the swastika, and how it sends chills up the back of my spine to see it, even to this day. And how I have learned that the Nazis did not create this symbol. They co-opted it from the people of the world, because there are swastikas in ancient cultures around the globe. It is one of the most ancient symbols of our primal spirituality, showing not only the elemental makeup of our being in the form of the cross but also the movement and dynamism of our makeup, symbolized by the tailing pieces at the end of each member of the cross. So even though the word *swastika* means blessing in Sanskrit, and even though it is a remarkable symbol of primal spirituality, it is almost impossible to use it for its original purpose because of the oppression of Nazi Germany and its co-opting of this sacred symbol.

In my own country, I think of the state of the black family in the United States. Even now, 150 years after the end of slavery, black families, and particularly black men, are still in the process of reclaiming their honor and their dignity. The way that welfare has tended to supplant the fathers of black families has not helped. This oppression has had an awful impact on the primal spirituality of black Africans whose ancestors were taken in slavery to America. People like Martin Luther King, Jr., Malcolm X, and Rosa Parks are among many African Americans who have helped the people of this nation—black, white, and of all colors— heal from this tragedy.

Oppression is present in the field of religion. One result of oppression is that the oppressed people are robbed of their names for God. Most people I know would not dare to create their own names for the Divine. They either accept the names given to them by their religion or they reject those names. But it would not enter their heads that they could have the audacity to find that special name for God that carries the tone and substance of their personal knowing of the Divine.

> *What is your name for the Divine?*
> *What name brings the most connection and*
> *resonance with the sacred for you?*

Following my workshop in Stroud, I traveled to Cape Town, South Africa, to present at a conference, "Activating Seeds of Destiny." African teacher, author, and dramatic artist Mmatshilo Motsei spoke to the audience about her concern that Christian religion was disempowering black Africans. It was easy to think that oppression could have robbed South Africans of their primal spirituality, and religion plays a part.

The conference was attended mostly by white South Africans, mostly of English descent. Is it possible that these people too carry the mark of oppression? In the South African context, they are more likely to be seen as the oppressors. But in the history of the English, there is huge oppression suffered by the people who now consider themselves English.

There was oppression by the Romans, the Vikings, and the Normans. There was the conquest of Northern Ireland, Scotland, and Wales, with many of those people becoming part of the English culture. Then there is the oppression of lower classes by upper classes that continues in some form to this day, and the oppressive boarding-school upbringing to which many English children are subjected.

It is more difficult to see someone who is in the role of an oppressor as someone who is suffering the results of oppression. But as one of the presenters at the Cape Town conference, Iris Canham-Gezane, wrote (*The Wounded Daughters of Africa,* page xvii):

Even a perpetrator is a victim too, a soul who has drifted far from home.

Sadly, oppression is like abuse. Those who have endured it are more likely to perpetrate it.

There is oppression of all kinds, and the subtler the oppression, the more difficult it is to become aware of and the more difficult it is to fight. In the United States, women's liberation was supposed to be a freedom movement. There have been many positive consequences of the movement. However, if you ask many woman, particularly single mothers, if they feel free trying to both raise a family and pursue a career, they might say no.

Meanwhile, children are fed to the mass media of our day. It looked good when it started—*Sesame Street* seemed to hold such promise with its teaching of the alphabet with television frames of a second or less. But *Sesame Street* soon gives way to MTV, endless video games, and social media, with children losing touch with the outdoors, play, and others. Then we wonder about attention deficit disorder. This is oppression of a different kind.

The Stockholm syndrome is the tendency for imprisoned, kidnapped, and especially tortured people to identify with their captors. This tendency in the human psyche is the only way I can explain the Tea Party—the ultraconservative movement in the United States. Generally speaking, the Tea Party is composed of less educated, less economically advantaged people in the more rural areas in Middle America. They are identifying with the interests of the rich—which they, on average, are not—and they are advocating for those interests, while the gap between rich and poor continues to widen. They are adopting a religious worldview that affirms their advocacy for those interests. That is the Stockholm syndrome at work in the world.

So I have come to believe that most of humanity is suffering from a psychology of oppression—even those who seem to be in the role of the oppressors. That it is because of that oppression that we have lost the knowledge of the most elemental aspects of our Being—who we are, our relationship to creation, and how our own human capacity works. There is a natural darkness that welcomes the light when it comes. But the darkness of oppression is not natural at all. It is a kind of darkness that hates the light. Rays of enlightened thought and enlightened awareness are the end of oppression, and those who are defending oppression know it.

It is time to regain primal spirituality—an innate knowing of ourselves. And if people look at me or you like we have two heads when we tell them about this, the problem is probably not with us. They might be suffering from the effects of oppression, playing the role of the perpetrator or the victim. Either way, have compassion. It might be time for you to bring the knowledge and empowerment of their primal spirituality. It might be time for you to shed light in those dark places.

How have you been oppressed in your life? How has it affected you? What would it take to free yourself from the impact of that oppression?

Four Virtues

I have always been suspicious about discussions of human virtue. So often, someone is trying to advance their pet beliefs about how other people should behave. My issues probably date back to early childhood when "being good" was not high on my list of priorities. I was more interested in finding out who I was and what my life was about. I have noticed that through my adult life, the admiration of supposed virtue has so often been shown toward people who seemed shallow, misdirected, and artificial—like the admiration of many movie stars and politicians. It has seemed to have more to do with someone's moralistic worldview and materialistic values than with the real virtues I respected in people I admired.

Recently, my in-depth exploration of primal spirituality has led me to identify qualities of experience that people enter into when spiritual gateways are open. I was surprised to find that we could name those experiences related to each of the four human capacities, and if we thought of those names in the largest context possible, they cover the entire human experience. Those names are *generosity, intelligence, strength,* and *flow.* As I thought further about it, these are experiences, but they are also virtues of a human being that transcend humanly defined morals or values. They are born out of Universal Being within each person.

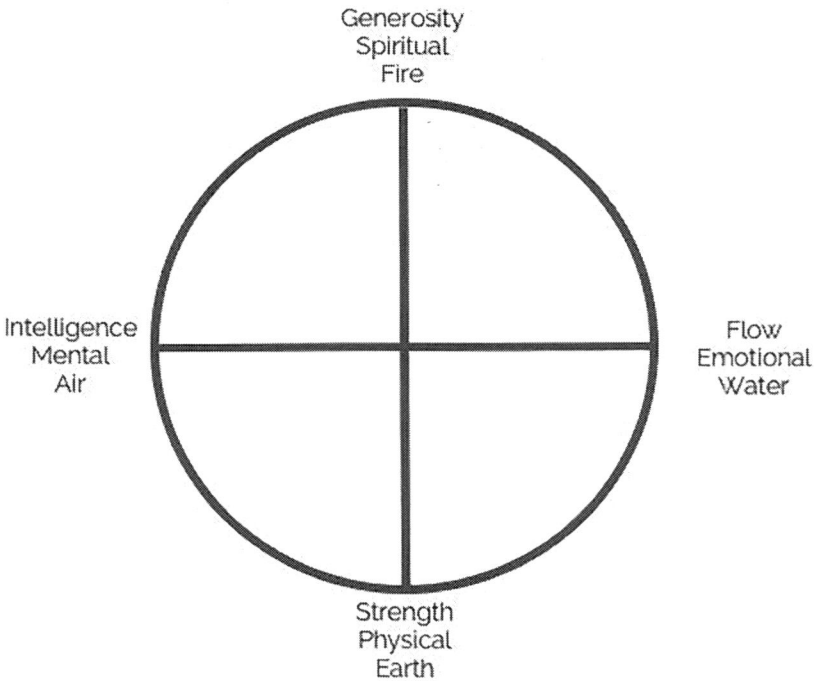

Four Virtues, Four Capacities, Four Cosmic Forces

In the illustration, there are names for the human embodiment of the four cosmic forces: water, air, earth, and fire—four aspects of the one creative spirit behind all creation and at work in human beings. And just like the four forces themselves, the virtues that are an embodiment of those forces are in dynamic relationship with one another.

Most of the Western world is still recovering from the limitations in consciousness that pervade most of the Judeo–Christian religious teachings of that world. Even though there can be great and wonderful truths presented through those teachings, they have often separated the sacred from the human, as if God were at work up in heaven, or at the dawn of time, or through Christ Jesus, but not through the human capacity. Even if a person has rejected those teachings, and the practice of the religion that goes with them, the damage has often been done. Reverence for the working of the spiritual directly in human experience is lost. And so the sense of wonder at the power of creation that moves through thoughts, feelings, and through the physical body is greatly diminished.

For some, there is the belief that God can work through a person as the holy spirit. So there is appreciation for the possibility that God, by whatever name, does not have to be so distant. The idea often associated with this belief is that all of who the human being is can open up to all that God is extending to them. This belief can be translated into an ecstatic experience, named by some as the "outpouring of the holy spirit."

Many forms of contemporary spirituality practiced in the West, whether they are born out of the Judeo–Christian context, Buddhism, Hinduism, or some other source, take a similar approach. As they conceive it, the individual human beings have the opportunity to open all of who they are to the Divine and all that the Divine has to extend to them. This approach takes people a step closer to real engagement with the creative spirit within them. However, the actual experience of that Divine working is far more complex for the individual than one human being activated by one creative spirit. That is not what it is like to have a daily experience of the Divine.

Some religious teachings liken the human being to a hollow reed. The implication is that if we could only get our humanity out of the way, the spirit could come through us. So just like Pentecostal Christians can achieve a heightened experience of the Holy Spirit during a church service, people who meditate can achieve a heightened spiritual experience of a different nature.

When it comes to the living of daily life, people from both these practices are faced with a far more complex human experience. If only it were so simple that God works everything out up in heaven—in an elevated reality far from our experience—and then hands His spirit, or

His consciousness, off to us. And then our only job is to open up to it and let it through. But that is not how daily life works for us as human beings on Planet Earth.

The creative spirit of the Divine is throwing a party inside of you. The four cosmic forces, which are part of that one creative spirit, have set up house in your humanity and they are relating dynamically to one another through your body, mind, emotions, and spirit. No wonder there is such chaos going on with most people! If only the spirit of the Divine were premade, then handed to you on a golden platter. But that is clearly not what is happening, at least not most of the time.

The truth is that four cosmic forces are engaging dynamically with one another through your four capacities, embodied as four virtues: the generosity of the spiritual, the intelligence of the mental, the strength of the physical, and the flow of the waters of the human heart. They are interacting dynamically within you and among you and other people. With your intelligence, you may be attempting to understand what is flowing in your emotions, or in the emotions of someone else. For example, this is the essential dynamic between a therapist or counselor and a client. Through the power moving through your spiritual body, you may offer a gift of love that touches someone else's heart. This is the essential dynamic between a mother and her baby, or between people who are falling in love. It is also the basis for self-love. You may use the strength of your physical experience to follow the intelligent plan someone devised mentally, as when a carpenter follows the blueprints created by an architect. And so it goes in the dynamic relationship among these elemental aspects of all people.

Is all this dynamism in the human experience a mistake? If you were expecting the Divine to be all peace and bliss, you would probably think so, but we are talking about the spirit that is creating planets and stars, rocks, trees, and sky. Looking at creation around us, it does not simply appear, premade, from another dimension. The creative wisdom and power that creates all things does appear from another dimension. It is all that and more.

Ultimately, creation is the result of dynamic relationships of cosmic forces at the level of the creation. Why should you be different? The embodiment of who you are is a result of the dynamic relationship among all the parts of who you are. As you flow with that dynamism, you experience creativity and joy. As you fight it—if what you are trying to accomplish is in conflict with that dynamism—you experience chaos. As actor and filmmaker Woody Allen said, "If you want to make God laugh, tell him about your plans."

What you are creating with other people is the result of the dynamic relationship brought to focus through parts of who you are and parts of who they are—your mind relating to their heart. The spiritual possibility you are carrying, inspiring their physical strength and stamina. And so it goes.

The ancients understood this dynamism and portrayed it through a graphic depiction of a cross in motion—one thing with four aspects in dynamic relationship that shift and evolve over time, with different dynamic relationships in focus at different stages of the creative process. This cross was found by Colonel James Churchward, a British-born author who traced its origin to an ancient civilization in the Pacific Ocean, known as Lemuria.

THE SACRED SYMBOLS OF MU

Tablet No. 1231

226

This cross is an ancient swastika that was used many thousands of years prior to Nazi Germany. Symbols like this can be found from ancient cultures around the globe.

The Creation story in Genesis 2:10 (KJB) tells how the godhead manifests in the world as one river that divides into four heads:

And a river went out of Eden to water the garden;
and from thence it was parted, and became into four heads.

Here is the ancients' description of the godhead—one reality manifesting through four streams of energy. You are being initiated into an experience of these energies every moment of your life. They are throwing a party inside you. The more the light of consciousness is shed on this event, the more you can enjoy the party.

How would your life change if you knew that your generosity,
intelligence, strength, and flow were gifts given to you by the universe
for the wonder of creation?

The Source of All Virtue

Generosity is the source of all virtue. Relative to any aspect of your experience, it is the knowing that you have more to give. When you bring generosity to your thinking, you have more ideas, more compassionate understanding, along with more beautiful plans and designs to manifest.

When you bring generosity to your feeling, you have more ability to respond to love, more openness, and more enthusiasm for what is manifesting in your life. When you bring generosity to your physical experience, you have more strength and endurance to fulfill your mission; you have more ability to act with precision and accuracy, and you bring more protection to the heart of love.

Your generosity creates a sense of abundance in your world. If you are in touch with the truth that there is more you have available to give within you, you soon have faith that creation provides. There is more than enough. There is abundance. There is light.

Sure, there are limits to anyone's internal resource—to their intelligence, strength, and flow. There are times when a person does not know what to do. Times when people run out of the strength and will to carry on, and they need a rest. And there are times when their heart feels so broken that they want to pull way back into themselves and stop themselves from flowing and connecting to anyone else.

That is where your spiritual capacity comes in. This is the source of your generosity. When you think you just can't go on, you find your generosity in surrender. As a song sung by a friend of mine declares, *I am strongest when I am on my knees.* True surrender is to the neverending resource of Universal Being, which always has more for you to give. Maybe not right now. Maybe after some needed rest and maybe after receiving what the world has to give back to you. And maybe not in the way you thought. But Universal Being always has more to give through you.

Think of what goes wrong in the human experience. We lose faith in our leaders when we believe that they lack generosity; when we believe they are not leading out of an attitude of pure service, but that they are more interested in taking than giving. Think of the serious issues that come up among you and other people in your life. At the heart of those issues, is there not a question of generosity? Or think of every person you have ever mentored or encouraged or assisted in any way in his or her life path. At the root of the challenges they faced, wasn't there a belief in the lack of their own internal resource? Perhaps a tendency to focus on their needs and what they weren't getting from the world?

The hard truth is that people cannot find their own generosity when they become obsessed with themselves—what they want, what they need, and what they believe they should have from the world and from other people. That obsession severs people's connections with their own internal resource of light and love. Their own lacks fill the screen of consciousness and their own internal resources become impossible to find.

This is self-centeredness—preoccupation with your human needs at the expense of generosity. Self-centeredness shuts down the flow of generosity to thinking, to feeling, and to the strength of the body and the strength of will. Without generosity, the virtues of intelligence, strength, and flow are blocked. What remains is ignorance, weakness, and rigidity, which are simply the lack of those virtues.

Generosity is the fuel for all virtues in the human experience. A sun is ever-generous. It shines unconditionally. You are becoming a sun when you find your generosity and let it light up your being.

Where are you focusing on what you are not getting from the world?
How can you be more generous?

Primal Spirituality, Table Mountain, and the White Lion

Primal spirituality is spirituality before religion. Before there ever was a religion, before there ever was a spiritual path or a spiritual journey, there was primal spirituality. It is the knowing of our Being, the knowing of who we are, the knowing of our place in the universe and our role as an embodiment of the Creator in Creation.

Primal spirituality is pristine spirituality. We often think of nature as being pristine. By definition, the Earth is a dirty place. And yet it is, at the same time, pristine, even with all its rotting leaves and other decaying plant life. Even with all the manure from all the animals. Nature is pristine.

The truth of the human experience is also pristine. But how many people really know it? Can you view your own emotional realm as pristine? There might be things rotting in there. There might be all kinds of storms and lots of transformation occurring. But just because there are storms and transformation in nature does not take away from the pristine quality of the natural world. The same is true for a human being.

I have been reviewing my own human experience and that of people that I meet. I have been reviewing the fact that for most people the function of their own humanity is a mystery to them. The workings of their own heart and mind often baffle them, and they feel great shame about what they think and feel. The knowing of who they are and their place in the world is mostly a mystery to them. Their relationship with the universe is a mystery. The primal spirituality that is the true normal for us as human beings has somehow been taken away—and there is instead a belief in a power and wisdom that is outside a person.

There is a belief in the power of big government and big business. There is belief in the power of the Illuminati Enlightenment-era societies believed, by some, to be at work in our world today, or in some other elite in hidden places. And for some, there is a belief in the power of aliens, astrology, or unembodied spiritual entities that determine the course of our lives.

There is faith in the knowledge held by the institutions of our world—the universities, the religions, and the scientific communities—and the belief that their knowledge is the most important knowledge and that for most of us it is impossible to possess it. For many, there is a belief in some almighty deity who holds all the power and does not give us any, and lords it over us, and then when we die decides how good or bad we have been, in his judgment, and sends us to heaven or hell, or sends us back to Earth for another try because we did not perform well this time.

I am not commenting on whether any of these things exist. I am questioning the deep-seated belief that there is something outside us that holds the wisdom and power that is the primary influence in our lives and that we, as human beings, do not. That is superstition, the ultimate enemy of primal spirituality in the human experience.

The Merriam-Webster dictionary defines superstition this way:

A belief or practice resulting from ignorance, fear of the unknown, trust in magic or chance, or a false conception of causation.

Any conception of causation that gives ultimate power to what is, for you, outside of you, is a false conception of causation, because the greatest power in our life is within us. Teachings of all kinds, from the academic and scientific to the philosophical, the religious, and the spiritual, often become teachings of disempowerment through which people learn to believe in a causation for their own life that is outside themselves and not within them and not accessible to them.

Even true teachings of primal spirituality get turned and twisted. Think of what Jesus said. "The kingdom of God is *within you*" (italics added, Luke 17:21, KJB). "The kingdom of heaven is *at hand*" (italics added, Matthew 4:17, KJB). Not later. Not after you die. Not in a power of any kind outside of you. Within you and at hand.

The truth is that the biggest factor in the fulfillment of a human life is the expression by that person of the potential that is within them. Any teaching that displaces a person's confidence in that potential with a "false conception of causation" for their life is superstition, no matter how rational it sounds. It is a disempowering teaching and it is not primal spirituality.

Primal spirituality brings people to an experience of their own power and wisdom. That experience confirms for us that if anyone or anything has taken our freedom, it is because we have given it up.

Any true teaching, and any true religion, is one that leads people to know the empowering truth within them and within all Creation.

The "Activating Seeds of Destiny" conference I attended in 2013 was held in Cape Town, South Africa. This place is called alternatively Cape of Storms and Cape of Good Hope. It is both. It didn't stop blowing while I was there. So it is the Cape of Storms, which I take to mean it is the Cape of Transformation. A storm transforms, and there certainly has been a storm of transformation occurring for people there. Because it is a Cape of Transformation, it is also the Cape of Good Hope. We stood at the foot of Africa, bringing transformation and therefore bringing good hope to the world.

During the conference, in the storytelling tradition of Africa, Iris Canham-Gezane shared this prophetic vision:

When the spirit of the white lion ascends Table Mountain
and proceeds from there, at the foot of Africa in the Cape, and
ascends up through this continent,
Africa will awaken to its primal spirituality. And when Africa awakens,
this whole world will awaken to a new experience for all humanity.

This story of the white lion is an allegory for the emergence of primal spirituality in all the world. This is what we are here to do—to bring the light to bear and awaken the primal spirituality of all people.

What are the storms that you are experiencing?
What is transforming for you?
How is this experience giving you hope?

All the Stupid Little Things

All the stupid little things
that so many people do!
Enough to make a strong man tired
on a bright and sunny morning.

May wisdom come to these people!
Let them forsake
all the twists and turns of the heart
that strangle a happy life
and make good people
agonize at noon
and leaves them desolate
as the sun sets
behind burnt, brown hills.

How I pray
for whatever potion it is
that cures a person
of their petulant insistence
on destroying the one opportunity
before them
to live a happy, fulfilled life.

Something You Give

Most often enlightenment is thought of as something to be received. And while there is some receiving involved, enlightenment is not primarily something that can be received. It is something you give. A person knows enlightenment as it is given. In whatever way a person might seek enlightenment, on that basis it is never found. You cannot *seek* enlightenment and find it.

The truth is that there is only one place from which enlightenment comes. It is the same place from which it has always come. It is ever available. It is cosmically available—the sun does not seem to be striving over this; neither are the other stars. It is constantly available for human beings to experience as well. However, there's only one way a human being can experience it, and that is *to be like the sun and to give it.*

I think if I were God, and I were creating a just world, I might create it like that. I might make it so that for people to experience the ultimate fulfillment of their life they would have to be generous in the giving of their light. I might make it so that they could not get it for themselves but so that they could only receive it if they would give it. That would strike me as a just and a fair way to make the world. The experience of enlightenment is the fulfillment of anyone's life.

People try to enlighten themselves about all kinds of things, looking at the world, looking at circumstances, looking at other people, maybe even looking into their own psyche. This approach is even taken with spiritual matters. There is a natural desire to try to find out what is going on and try to make it work. This is the engineering mind at work. I do not want to put down engineers, because there is a place for engineers and the engineering mind, and the tendency to think that if we just put it all together in our minds, things would all work. If we did not figure it out this time, maybe we will get it right the next. But this thinking doesn't always work in the creative process of becoming a sun.

For human beings, the most significant light in their life is the light they give, not the light they receive. And the act of seeing is not just an act of receiving what is coming from our world. It is a giving act; it is a creative act. We paint the world with our spirit, and our spirit is carried on the current of our seeing. Have you ever noticed that? We can wake up in the morning and feel the wonders of the day and therefore see them. But when there is something else going on in the heart, if there's a disturbance of the heart, there is no radiant feeling and thinking.

Martin Cecil, who wrote and taught on the spiritual destiny of humanity, said this in a 1979 service he gave, titled "The Light of Illumination," about the opportunity a person has to illuminate their world:

> *The size of the world for each one is based in the extent of vision, one's own vision; and the quality of one's world is dependent upon the quality of one's own living. The extent of vision will in turn depend upon the extent of the light that is shining, the intensity of that light.*

Russian writer, philosopher, and social activist Leo Tolstoy said this in *Thoughts of Prince Andrew*, Book 12, chapter 16, on the topic:

> *All, everything that I understand, I understand only because I love. Everything is, everything exists, only because I love. Everything is united by it alone. Love is God.*

Love is God. Not the God of religion. But the God of creation. The vibration of love through people is the creator for their world. That vibration of love coming through us is creating our world every day. The nature of the world that is created, the extent of it, depends on the quality of vibration that is coming through us. We could call some range of that vibration love; we could call another range of it light. It is all the creative vibration that comes through a person, to whatever degree. Where it comes through generously and fully and clearly, it lights up our world. We can see. Do you think that might be enlightenment?

When a person has a deep and genuine desire to be nourished spiritually and to understand, the kindest thing to do is to show them, as quickly as one can, where the source of that lies. This was at the core of what Jesus taught. It came out in his teachings this way:

The kingdom of God is within you (Luke 17:21, KJB).

And in this great teaching:

I have meat to eat that ye know not of . . .
My meat is to do the will of him that sent me, and to finish his work
(John 4:32, 34, KJB).

The finishing is about letting what is within come all the way out, so that it reaches the people around you and fills your world. That is the finishing.

These words of Krishna from Chapter 2 of the Bhagavad-Gita carry the same message:

The mind of pure devotion—even here—
Casts equally aside good deeds and bad,
Passing above them. Unto pure devotion
Devote thyself: with perfect meditation
Comes perfect act, and the righthearted rise—
More certainly because they seek no gain—
Forth from the bands of the outer, step by step,
To highest seats of bliss. When thy firm soul
Hath shaken off those tangled oracles
Which ignorantly guide, then shall it soar
To high neglect of what's denied or said,
This way or that, in doctrinal writ.
Troubled no longer by the priestly lore,
Safe shall it live, and sure; steadfastly bent
On meditation. This is Yog—and Peace!

The highest spiritual teaching points to this truth: enlightenment is something you give. It comes from within you.

Find a simple way to bring an enlightened thought
to someone in your world.

Entering Your Own Solitude

We have the opportunity to open the door to another reality—to enter an experience that goes beyond the common experience in the world in which we live. To open a door to another reality for our world and the people in it, we have to open that door *from* another reality. As we embrace our knowing of a place of being that transcends the everyday experience of people, and even our own everyday experience, we have the opportunity to open a door from that place and let that reality express and deepen through ourselves and then into the world.

You may hope for or expect something wonderful, perhaps something spiritual, to happen in your life, ascending to greater and greater heights of spiritual awareness. But the spiritual journey is not just a journey of going up. It is not only a journey of ascension. It is also a journey of coming down—descending. To continue on your journey, you have to let the reality of your Being come down from the highest place within yourself through you and out into the world.

The journey to that experience is full of so many things, and our humanity gets to experience them all. My own experience includes an embrace of solitude. I expect that is true for you too—that for you to enter into the joy of creation fully, to come to a place where you can allow the expression of who you are to deepen in and through you and to open a door from another reality, there does have to be an embracing of your own solitude. It is an experience of moving away from the crowd, moving away from the comfort of rubbing shoulders with others.

For me, there is something reassuring about the jocularity I share with other men. I enjoy the familiarity of comradeship and friendship, and there is an assurance within all that, that I am doing okay, and it's all right and it's all familiar. And all of that is wonderful.

But I know my own journey has called me to what seems initially like a place of loneliness, solitude, and singularity. Ultimately, I have to rely on my highest perception of what is true. And in that, I have to receive a confirmation that does not come from the pats on the back offered by people or the familiarity of being with other people.

Real confirmation comes from the highest place within me. At the end of this cycle, whatever the cycle is and whatever an end looks like, as I face my own knowing of what is true, what will matter will be my ability to say, "Yes, I've done what was mine to do; I've expressed what was mine to express; I've brought the gift that was mine to give; I've shared my light; and I've lived the life that was mine to live; and most of all, I have served that reality that I came here to serve"—that is the test of the fulfillment of a cycle.

This is also what allows me or anyone to bring what would be my greatest gift to my world and to other people. All the jocularity and need for familiarity and approval takes away from what we know when we walk through the door that initially looks like loneliness and solitude, but that ends up being a door into an experience of supreme focus within oneself. It is an experience of receiving, embracing, and bringing into the world the greatest gift we have to give.

There is an expression about leadership that goes something like this: It's lonely at the top. People who lead often have that experience, at least at times. Yet we are all born to lead, and we all belong at the top in our world, and we all have a calling to walk through a door that looks like loneliness and solitude. It does not actually end up that way, because if you embrace that for yourself, you find that there is presence in that solitude. There is not just loneliness. And one of the gifts of being alone is finding that you are not. You are never alone.

In one of Martin Luther King, Jr.'s most moving speeches, he talked about his experience of this. He was speaking about facing the great challenges during the Montgomery, Alabama, bus boycott:

I could hear the quiet assurance of an inner voice saying: "Martin Luther, stand up for righteousness. Stand up for justice. Stand up for truth. And lo, I will be with you. Even until the end of the world."...

I heard the voice of Jesus saying still to fight on . . .

He promised never to leave me alone. . . Almost at once my fears began to go. My uncertainty disappeared.

~ *The Autobiography of Martin Luther King, Jr.,* chapter 8 ~

When we come to a place of serving the highest reality we know, that highest reality is with us; the presence of that reality is there and never, ever lets us down. It is always there to bring the gift of the moment; it's always available to call on. And if there is a challenge in a circumstance, there is always a greater love in that presence for you to bring to that circumstance. And if there is something confounding in your life, there is always a greater wisdom available that sees more than you have yet seen.

In giving that greater love and wisdom expression in life, it is likely that enlightened people will annoy a few other people and they will end up turning some people away. There are not too many who embrace their own solitude who have the same friends when they come out the other end as when they went in. You have to be ready to have a different kind of relationship with the people in your world when you wear the crown that is rightly yours to wear. Because whatever relationship you have had with the people in your world, you now have a different relationship.

However your outer roles might appear, they are now in your kingdom if you accept that reality for yourself. They are now part of that reality that you are knowing for yourself, so they are now included in that reality. They have become one of your people. And whatever they do, however wonderful, however dramatic, however inscrutable, however nonsensical, neither they nor you can change that reality unless you are willing to take your crown off your head and live a different life.

My experience is that all the familiarity and comradeship of the familiar world that I knew does not begin to touch the love and friendship that I know with people who unabashedly wear their crown, with people who have unabashedly walked through a doorway into a different experience, and who therefore are themselves in position to open a door from another reality. There is a door to walk through to enter that experience. Biblically, the experience of another world was spoken of as the Garden of Eden, with an entrance guarded by cherubim, who held flaming swords.

I have a simpler way of describing the door to another world of experience. The door is selflessness. And there is no real selflessness without selfless service to a higher reality. I am not talking about charitable works here, per se, as noble as charitable works might be. You could do many charitable works and not pass through this door. Walking through this door, you know the reality of love, which brings oneness. You know beauty unspeakable. You have the opportunity of reclaiming or, to use a religious term, redeeming your own humanity. You have the opportunity to redeem your own soul for the deepening expression of yourself and the reality you know.

If you are facing a door in your life that looks like solitude, these words might strike you as somber or grave. Solitude can look like that. Yet within that solitude is light, freedom, and joy. Embracing your own solitude, you are free. You find the source of your happiness and joy. You find the greatest gift you have to bring to the world.

Learn to be with yourself and enjoy your own company. Embrace your own loneliness and the opportunities you have to be alone. And discover that you are never alone.

I invite you to enter fully into your own solitude and, in so doing, inherit the wonder of creation, the creative power of the truth of love, set free through the doorway that you are to your world.

How could you spend more time with the light within you?

Chapter Six

THE GRAVITY

OF

COURAGE

Your time is limited, so don't waste it living someone else's life.
Don't be trapped by dogma—which is living with the results of
other people's thinking.

Don't let the noise of others' opinions drown out your
own inner voice.

And most important, have the courage to follow your
heart and intuition.

~ STEVE JOBS ~

Selfhood

Selfhood is an elusive concept. After all, what is a self? It is like the concept of "the observer" in quantum physics. You can search the human anatomy and you won't find it. The evidence of its presence is found throughout the human psyche but, look as you might, you won't find it there. Yet we know the qualities of selfhood when we see them embodied in someone's life.

The reason you cannot find the self is simply because you *are* the self. It makes no sense to look for who you are. You can only *be* who you are.

In its purest essence, selfhood is presence. Self is a point of position with no magnitude. The purest statement of the self in English is *I am.* Or in Sanskrit, *Aum.*

As you become a sun, you are embodying the self that you are. Your humanity is becoming you more and more fully. To allow that to happen, you have been building your human capacity to embody and express who you are. That building is the human journey, individually and collectively.

We are all creating a human capacity to embody and express the self. For most people, the human capacity never fully reveals the self within it. And the fractured state of humanity as a whole has not yet allowed the glory of being within it to be clearly revealed, even though the glory of what is within people shows itself in all kinds of ways.

What are the attributes of an embodied experience of self? If you were going to build a flesh body you were going to incarnate into, what would those attributes be? There have to be qualities and abilities that set you free to express yourself through that flesh body. Here is a beginning list of the attributes of a human soul who has the capacity to express selfhood:

- Choice
- Will
- Pleasure
- Uniqueness
- Power
- Creativity

It takes these qualities for a person to create a world—their world. When you embrace your own selfhood, you are creating a world that is uniquely yours. All the people in that world live in the reach of your solar wind—in your heliosphere. As you are a whole person, you are creating a whole world.

Any chance for trouble here? Of course there is. As human beings, we can make poor choices. Our will can lead us to behavior that is antagonistic to others and to the world around us. The ability to experience pleasure can lead to addiction and narcissism. The attributes that allow us to experience who we are in human form carry strong risks. This is particularly true for people enmeshed in the swirl of their thinking and feeling, who are not living in their own clear presence as a being.

At this point in your process of becoming a sun, embrace these attributes of your humanity. You have to if you desire to be a whole person. Your courage to embrace all the qualities of selfhood brings the gravity of the sun who you are. Your courage allows you to be at the center of your solar system, holding all that is revolving around you in its orbit with your gravitational pull. There is a time to embrace every part of who you are, and, in embracing it, make it your own. Only you know if now is that time.

It might have seemed that being a good person or being spiritual meant that you avoided some of these qualities of selfhood. You might be trying to be selfless, which can be a noble endeavor. Some teachings suggest that we should be like a hollow reed. No self, just an open channel for the spiritual to pour through us. That can be a good strategy for a stage in a person's life. For some, that stage lasts a lifetime. However, for many, there is a call to do more.

If you have undergone the creative process portrayed in this book, you are now ready to be more than an open channel for Universal Being to pour through. You are ready to *be* Universal Being and to pour through your humanity. You are the Being who is ready to embrace the human instrument you have created, to exercise your choice and your will, your power, and your creativity. It's all for your pleasure and fulfillment as a unique aspect of the whole of Universal Being.

How can you embrace more fully the attributes of humanity?
Choice? Will? Pleasure? Uniqueness? Power? Creativity?
What would that look like in your life?

Being Yourself

The journey to a fulfilled life begins when you live into the wonder of what is possible for you to experience and create. It includes an opening to an awareness of the wonder of Being within you and the vastness of Universal Being—the spiritual reality within all Creation. The journey also leads you to aspire to create your own world of wonder—a place in which the possibility that you have touched can thrive. These are the steps that have been portrayed in the first five chapters of this book. They are all steps on the journey to becoming a sun.

On this journey, it often seems like the goal is to embrace a state of being that is something other than you and to let that reality live in the world around you. That perspective on the process is necessary because it introduces new inspiration and wisdom to your human experience. It has let you see and know things you could not have known any other way. However, your journey is not complete until you have a radical change in your approach to life. That change is *from* the perspective of a person who seeks an experience of being that is outside themselves *to* an experience of being that is incarnating through their humanity. It is an experience of *being* that Being who has chosen to incarnate in your humanity—in the person who you probably identify by the use of your own name.

This step is radical because it is the movement out of the belief that you have to change. Think about all the efforts you have made to grow, to learn, and to form new habits or behaviors. Think about all the discipline you have applied in your life to become a better person, a more knowledgeable person, and a more lovable person. Think about all the ways you have sought a more enlightened or a more loving experience.

No doubt, all those efforts played their part in your life journey. They might still. But it is hard to make that much effort over as many years as you have been making it without adopting a belief that there is something wrong with you—something that needs to change. And, more important, that you are what needs to change. That's not exactly self-affirming!

After all the effort to change personally, is it possible that who you really are does not need to change? Is it possible that you are already the wholeness of what you have been attempting to become? And that the true reason behind all your efforts is simply to embody and express who you are in the flesh of your body and through your thoughts and feelings?

This is not only possible, it is true. It is so true that I believe I can prove it to you right now. That proof is easy because all I have to do is call to your attention your own immediate experience in this present moment.

In the English language, the quintessential statement of Being is *I am.* Before you have thought a thought, felt a feeling, or taken an action, you have this experience. *I am.* It seems easy to qualify that experience with thought, feeling, and action to say, "I am worried," "I am sad," or "I am walking." But before you experience anything else, you have the experience expressed in these two simple words: *I am.*

If you stay with that experience for even a few short moments, you will easily begin to become aware of your own presence in the midst of whatever else might be happening in your life. You don't have to think, feel, or do anything to be you. You *are* that presence. You are a focused presence of Being in the world. Your presence is a point of position without magnitude that you are embodying through your humanity—through your mind, your emotions, and your physical body.

From that perspective, you are witness to your thoughts. You are also the origin of those thoughts. They are emanating from you. They come from you—your wisdom, your intelligence, and your understanding.

You are witness to your feelings. You are also the origin of those feelings. They too are emanating from you. They are expressing your love and your desire into the world.

Your thoughts and feelings are the dual channels of your conscious awareness. They provide the instrument through which you initiate action in the world. The thoughts and feelings of your conscious awareness are your means of embodying who you are in your physical body and expressing who you are in the world.

You are a perfect Being of love. You do not need to change. Your consciousness will change and grow and heal and evolve as you express through it. Your body will thrive as that happens. It will express who you are, and the gravity and magnitude of your love will manifest in your world.

You are already a sun. Your humanity is becoming a sun—a radiant expression of you in the world.

As you reflect on your own direct, personal experience, is this not what is happening? Your Being is expressing through your thoughts and feelings, and because of that your Being is filling your body and the world around you.

This ancient sun cross portrays many things, depending on the perspective from which you view it. From your perspective as the perfect Being who you are, it looks like this:

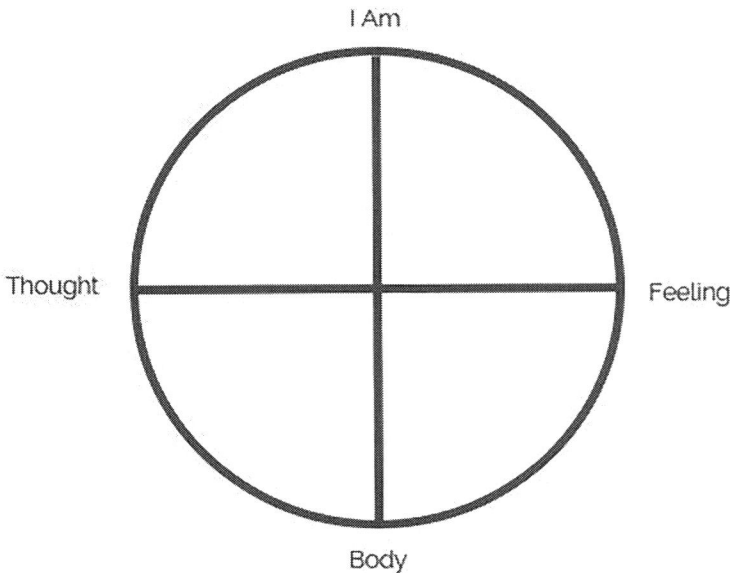

You could do your best to prove me wrong. You could adhere to a belief about who you are and what it is like to be you that contradicts me. But the chances are good that you are on a journey that is taking you to a deeper awareness of who you are as a Being, so that you can appreciate, more and more, your opportunity to express who you are through your human experience.

From that perspective, you can see the human tendency to be identified in a swirl of thoughts, feelings, and physical experience. The best of that experience aspires to experience the spiritual—to know God, to know enlightenment, or simply to lead a good life. Seldom does the consciousness of a person arise out of that swirl to a consistent awareness of the presence of their own Being. Consistent awareness leads to consistent embodiment. It leads to becoming a sun.

If you are having this experience, appreciate the fact that you are on the leading edge of what is breaking through in human consciousness today. Your awareness is a gift to share with others.

Are you being you, or are you trying to change or become you?
What if you just allowed yourself to be you?

Courage

The root of the word *courage* is from a French word for "heart." Courage is embodied by people when what flows from their heart supports their effort to be strong and when their strength protects their heart. So the virtue of courage is created by the joining of the virtues of flow and strength.

In archetypal terms, there is courage when the heart of the Lover flows to the strength of the Warrior, as expressed in the terms cf Moore and Gillette.

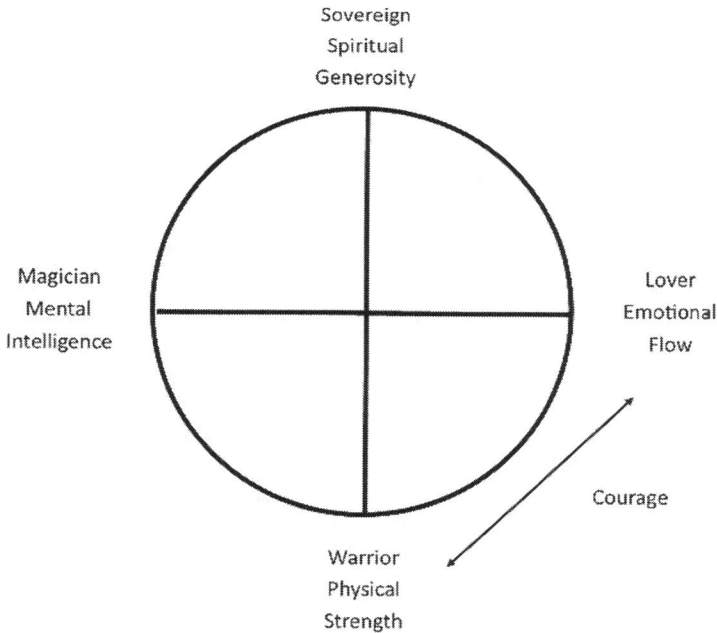

Behind the expression of courage is a matter of the heart. It is easy to express courage on the outside when your heart is given on the inside to the action you are taking.

Poet Maya Angelou said this about courage:

Courage is the most important of all the virtues,
because without courage you can't practice any other virtue consistently.
You can practice any virtue erratically, but nothing consistently
without courage.

~ Diversity: Leaders Not Labels ~

The most obvious form of courage is the courage to act. You might think of acts of bravery, such as the selfless efforts of the first responders at the World Trade Center on 9/11, who gave their lives that others might live during the horrific events. But courage in action might be far more common and far less dramatic. Like a mother who works two jobs while raising her family—for years. Or the courage of speaking up to support another person when the rest of the world is condemning and criticizing.

There is also the courage to think for yourself. It takes courage to have enough faith in your own intelligence not to simply accept what other people or the media believe, but to understand something deeply for yourself and then live based on that understanding. It takes courage to be brilliant in your thinking.

It takes courage to love. Your love might not be returned by the person to whom it is offered. You might even be ridiculed for the way you love. It takes courage to love anyway.

It takes courage to be yourself— to embrace your own humanity, perhaps broken and imperfect as it is. To embody and express who you are and let the world know you—that takes real courage.

Courage is the willingness to actually do it—to be your own cheerleader and put all your heart into who and what you are as a human being. To take that wild, committed leap to being yourself. Your courage brings the gravity of the sun that you are.

So what do you need courage for today? Can you be a cheerleader for yourself? Can you love who you are as a Being of action? Yes, you can. And today is the day. This is your time. You are a great person who has great things to do. You are a Being of love who has love to give to the world. You are a brilliant mind who has insights and vision to bring to the world. People have been waiting to meet who you are on the inside, and today is the day for you to express yourself as you never have before.

Join me in being a cheerleader for you.

What act of courage are you ready to do in your life now?
What will it look like for you to be your own cheerleader?

A Test of Heart and Soul

My courage to be myself and to do what is mine to do has certainly been tested in my life. One such test occurred in 1994 when I was president of a nonprofit organization in New York. There was a community of people involved who put on public events and offered programs for personal development and spiritual learning.

There came a time when the people leading the programs became disillusioned and, of course, their disillusionment influenced all of the participants. With a lack of leadership in an organization, there is often a power vacuum created, and that was certainly true in this case. The membership of the organization convened a series of meetings and dubbed the attendees at the meeting the "governing body." That was puzzling to me because I thought that the board over which I presided was the governing body of the organization.

I was living in Connecticut at the time, and I was doing financial work for IBM Credit Corporation in Stamford, Connecticut. I worked for the credit department, which was reeling from losses brought on by a recession related to the savings-and-loan crisis. Our department was implementing a new credit approval process and trying to stem losses from leases and loans to failing companies. IBM brought in a banker from Credit Suisse to lead the effort. The hours were long. But it was exhilarating to me. It challenged my creative thinking and my endurance.

For weeks, I drove, after work, from Connecticut to Long Island to attend the sessions of the self-proclaimed "governing body." The group members felt the void of leadership deeply, though no one seemed to know that this was the issue. The demands became louder and louder that someone satisfy their emotional and spiritual needs. Emotional outbursts and emotional processing became the order of the day. It went so far that one evening, a woman gained the attention of the group and told a gripping story of abuse. Only after the story was over did she reveal that the story was from a previous lifetime.

I remember thinking, *This will never end.*

Meanwhile, the board meetings were absorbed with demands from people that the financial resources of the organization be used to support the members, and some of my closest friends were involved. I knew that this would be a violation of the mission and purpose of the organization and a violation of trust with the people who donated to the organization. It was also illegal. Yet this did not seem to bother the other board members as it did me.

The time came for an election of the board. The "governing body" met to hear from the candidates, and it quickly became political. After I made my speech, a man who had been a close friend and was probably the most well-liked person in the community, stood up and asked me this, "Do you commit to do the will of the governing body? Do you commit to vote in favor of anything that the governing body approves?"

Everything in me knew that this was a pivotal moment.

I know what they want me to say—what they are demanding I say.
I know the "right answer": Consensus.
If I say yes, then I'll either be walking away from my legal and ethical responsibility as a member of this board, or I'll be committing to do something that I don't really intend to do.
I'd be lying. I can't believe they are doing this. I'm trapped.

"No, I can't promise that."

I knew that a board member has the responsibility to vote according to his highest awareness of what is in the best interest of the organization. And a vote of the "governing body" could never alleviate me of that responsibility.

I wasn't elected. It was a dreary ride, late that night, over the Throgs Neck Bridge back to Stamford.

A board member told me later that the friend who had challenged me said that I had shot myself in the foot, to which he replied, "It looked to me like *you* were the one who did the shooting."

For weeks, it felt like a bomb had detonated inside me. As I saw it, there was nothing I could do about what had happened. There was nothing to say that would do any good—no public statement that would make any difference. I believed that any appeal to the friend who had betrayed me would be to no avail. I had no interest in retribution or revenge.

The explosion inside continued to do its work. I felt terribly alone, with hardly a friend in the world. Energetically, the impact rattled around in my body and seemed to explode out the top of my head. In a way I had never known before, I felt connected to an invisible reality above me that was there for me, holding me steady in the midst of the personal crisis.

A month later, while sitting at my desk, at home in Stamford, I received a phone call. It was the leader of a nonprofit organization of global scope. He wanted to know if I would be open to be a member of their board.

"Yes!"

The test of heart and soul comes, of our courage to be true to ourselves, in many ways. This was a huge test in my life. It demanded that I think for myself—that I ponder deeply the ethics of a circumstance based on my highest values in the face of the mob psychology that had taken over. It demanded that I reach my own conclusions and then act on them. It required me to show up in my life as who I am—at the moment of crisis and in the days to come, regardless of the outcome. And, in this case, it required grieving a loss as a result before a new opportunity came along.

Courage is a habit. When you discover that you can live your life being true to yourself, nothing else will do.

The Initial Shock of Facing Your Humanity

If you are in the swirl of your thinking and feeling, you are seeing everything from that perspective. What is swirling for you right now? If you are unconscious of it, it will condition what you see. You will see the world around you from that perspective. You will also see whatever it is to which you aspire from that perspective. Your aspiration could be a desire for something different to manifest in your life. It could be something you consider spiritual.

As long as you are enmeshed in the swirl of your thinking and feeling, your vision will be influenced by your present experience. That is why, for some, the vision of spiritual reality is so strange—an angry God demanding vengeance. A spiritual reality that condemns people to hell or to endless reincarnation with endless suffering—unless they are good.

It is common for people to project their own experience—their own thoughts and feelings—on other people and the world around them. For instance, if they are caught in fearful thoughts and feelings they might see another person as threatening, even if the facts do not support that view. This is a dark shadow that is projected on someone else. Or they might adore another person because they are looking for the goodness they cannot find in themselves. Most celebrity adoration is based on this principle—people admiring someone beautiful, sexy, noble, or passionate when they cannot see those qualities in their own experience. This is a light shadow projected on another.

As long as you are identified with the swirl of thought and feeling, you will tend to be unaware of the profound impact that this swirl has on your view of reality. Just as you cannot see yourself without the aid of a mirror, when you are what you are thinking and feeling, you cannot see those thoughts and feelings clearly. You have the experience of being identified with them, but you have no perspective with which to see them for what they are.

This is so common that you might consider it normal. Most people hardly notice what is happening within themselves until it gets so extreme that it clearly requires some kind of significant reining in.

When you move out of the swirl of thought and feeling into an experience of the Being who you are, you are then in position to witness your thoughts and feelings like you never have before. You see the embodiment of yourself through you own thoughts, feelings, and actions. You are bringing the peace of your presence to your conscious awareness. And even if your thoughts and feelings are swirling, you know what is happening, and you have the courage to embrace that experience, not ignoring or running away from it. And through the courage to embrace all of your human experience, all of who you are shows up in the world. Your courage brings the gravity of who you are into the world.

This radical shift in perspective creates a radically different relationship with your mind and emotions. You can see them now. You can understand them. You can love them. You can embrace them.

This is the difference between looking for something to make you feel better and embracing how you actually feel. The difference is between aspiring to have a better experience and being thankful for the experience you have. The difference is between running away from the unresolved in your own heart and courageously embracing it like you never have before. The difference is between assuming you are a good person and knowing that you are neither good nor bad; you are just you—the presence of Being in human form.

Often, when people are making this radical shift, they experience shock and horror when they realize what has been happening in their minds and emotions. Or when they see actions they have taken in the past. They are becoming aware, for the first time, of how they have been criticizing other people for the same limitations they now see in themselves. They see how they have been trying to alleviate the unhappiness they feel inside by getting people and circumstances outside to give them joy. You might feel shame and disgust when you catch yourself acting out of your own internal disturbance. Can you stay present? Can you endure the feeling? Hold on. It might be a wild ride to begin with.

What allows a person to maintain this radical shift while experiencing this kind of shock is a radical strategy. That strategy is to face whatever awfulness you find in yourself and embrace it. Not to condone it. Not to become it. Not to keep it alive forever. Embrace whatever you see in yourself so that you can bring healing to it. So that you can accept that whatever it is, because it is in your house of Being. It is part of you. It was created out of you, no matter how distorted it became.

You are its creator, and therefore you are its master. You express your mastery through your presence. With your presence comes your love, and with your love comes your dominion. Your dominion extends to your thoughts and feelings because you are present. You see and you love.

Now your thoughts and feelings are truly yours. They are becoming available for the expression of your love and your wisdom—your blessing and your intelligence. They are the medium of consciousness through which you are embodying who you are. You are now owning your humanity.

The typical reaction for most people first experiencing this level of awareness is taken right out of the script from *Mission Impossible*, the popular TV show and movie series:

As always, should you or any of your IM Force be caught or killed,
the secretary will disavow any knowledge of your actions. Good luck, Jim.

Often, when the person is caught in the middle of an act, thought, or feeling that betrays their own inner turmoil, they would rather die than acknowledge what has been happening.

This radical shift is a reversal of that strategy. While experiencing the presence of Being, which is who you are, you are seeing and acknowledging, mostly to yourself, what is transpiring in your own thoughts and feelings. And if you have lost consciousness of the presence of Being, and acted out of the swirl of your mind and emotions, you see it for what it is and take responsibility for it—by loving yourself.

This is from an African story told by a South African, Iris Canham-Gezane.

> *In some tribes, before an African mother conceives, she listens for the song of the being to come. She teaches the song to the child. And if the child, at any age, performs a destructive act, the tribe members place the child in the middle of their circle and sing the song to them. To remind them of who they are. To remind them of their greatness. To assist them to embody who they are in their thoughts, their feelings, and their actions.*

This is part of a radical strategy for owning our humanity. If you can love your own humanity in this way, then you can love other people. This is one of the meanings of this essential teaching of Jesus, found in Matthew 22:39, KJB:

> *Thou shalt love thy neighbour as thyself.*

This is a compassionate, forgiving, transforming kind of love. It is unconditional love. It is the love of our Being for the humanity we created. As you exercise the courage to embrace your humanity, you might at times experience yourself in an almost excruciating kind of way. But that experience turns to love. If you have been trying to be spiritual, you will realize how human you are.

Your humanity will begin to embody who you are as a spirit as it never has before. Your dreams now have a chance to become a reality because you have the gravity to let them be fulfilled. You are being a sun. Your humanity is becoming a sun. And you are building a sun with the people in your world.

> *What thoughts and feelings are longing to be embraced?*
> *How can you show love to them?*

Yearning

There is a yearning
so deep in the heart
that it seldom shows itself
as it is.
On bad days
it is infatuation
or maybe lust.
Or the craziness
that befalls a man
when he smells
the musky scent
of the place he lives.
It is a bond
between two parts
of one thing
and the law established
by the god
who rules all relationships.
So we call it yearning or love
when it is the order of things
which has been set
in a heaven we hardly know.

And the best we can do
is to stop playing with the temptation
of knowing love as we never have before
and embrace what has been ordained for us
since the beginning of the world.

Water and Stone

Truly spiritual people are not only seeking a spiritual experience. They are having a spiritual experience, and they are embodying that experience as fully as possible in their lives. They are building a body of love. Our human soul cries out for the spirit to enter consciousness fully and express through thought, feeling, word, and action. The Being who is the truth of who you are longs to enter your soul and to enter the world in which you live.

It takes courage to come to the place of recognition that you are not just the soul who is looking for a spiritual experience. You are universal love, looking for a body, looking for the opportunity to express yourself in the most accurate and the most powerful way for this circumstance.

The body of love is a stone cut out without hands. Think of the way love is embodied in your own life—the love you share with those closest to you, or the love you share with the community of people that is around you. If you truly experience a body of love with other people, it was not created out of any kind of manipulation. A body of real love shared by people is built in one way, and one way only—through the clear expression of love over time. The wonder of love creates it. It is like a stone cut out without hands.

A stone has solidity and gravity. When the body of love is known among people, it is like that. They are solid as individuals and they have solidarity as a group. They possess the quality of gravity—*gravitas*! What they bring to the world has significance and weight. People who have the gravity of the sun attract to themselves all that is meant to be in their orbit. All that is meant to come to them to fuel their radiance—the people, the resources, the events, and the finances.

Who wouldn't want to have these qualities in their human experience? People have looked for the instruction manual. Leaders of all kinds have looked for the gravitas that would bring a group of people together to have the solidarity that would let them accomplish something. Parents try to hold families together. Business leaders try to bring the people of their organization together. Political leaders attempt to galvanize a political party.

While there might be some level of apparent success in any of these endeavors, it is only the real body of love known in the human experience that has the true gravity that holds people together. And the only way the body of love is created is by love itself, expressing clearly and consistently over time through individuals.

The expression of love is fluid. It is like water poured from a pitcher into a glass, taking the shape of that glass. The circumstance is the glass. When a person lets love pour through them accurately, it takes just the right shape for that circumstance. Love wants to find just what is needed. It wants to find the optimal action. It wants to engage with what is present right now in the most loving, the most creative, the most effective, and the most powerful way.

Assurance is the knowing that you are not just a human soul looking for a spiritual experience. You are a divine Being, seeking to embody the love that you are in the world. An assured person is allowing the flow of love to occur all the time. They are letting their love conform exactly to the shape of the circumstance. Without assurance, a person worries that if they did this, they would not be themselves. They might be two-faced if they said just what someone needed to hear. They might be inauthentic if they did not act in the same way they had always acted in a similar circumstance. They might be a doormat if they did not get what they wanted from other people.

What assured people know is they could not stop being themselves if they wanted to. When it comes to being who they are, they have nothing to prove. They are free to let their love flow as accurately and as clearly as possible into the circumstance. They are building a body of love in the world.

It seems like a paradox. Love is both the fluid expression in every moment and a reality that has the solidity and weight of a stone. Both these elements—fluidity and solidity—are essential factors in our physical body. Our bodies are mostly water and the bodily fluids are a necessary part of our physical function.

However, we need the structure of our skeletal system to hold us upright, to protect our internal organs and to keep us from flopping all over the place. The minerals necessary for the building of the skeletal system are carried through blood that flows in the circulatory system. Altogether, the appearance on the outside of our human bodies is of something solid, while we are mostly liquid inside.

These realities in our physical body are a manifestation of what is happening at other levels of our being. At a spiritual level, the fluid expression of love over time is what builds the solidity of the body of love that is present in any moment. Inside, there is the flow of love, embodied on the outside as love in solid form.

This relationship between what is solid and what is fluid in a person is the relationship between earth and water. It is the relationship between the flow of the emotional body and the strength of the physical body. Usually, for a person to understand how these seemingly opposite virtues work together, all of the other dynamics of a whole person have to be in place. The virtue that is embodied when the flow of the emotional body engages with the strength of the physical body is courage.

Your courage brings the gravity of the sun to your world.

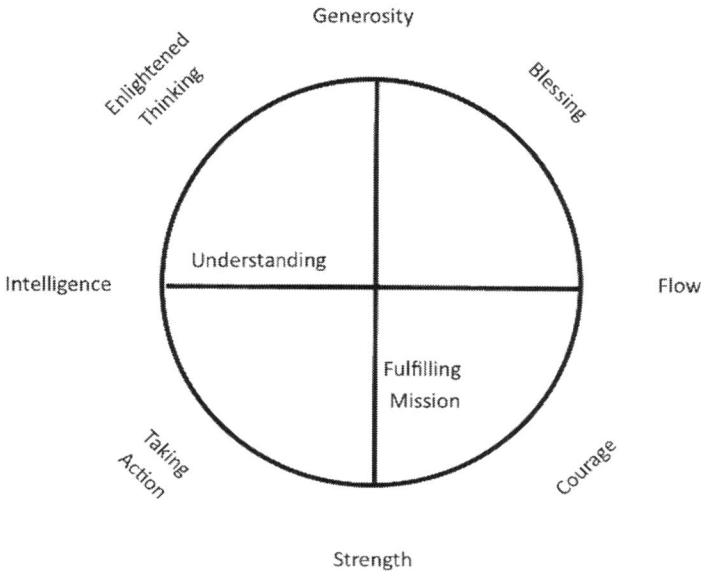

In our human life there has to be fluidity so that we can assume whatever structure and whatever shape is right for us to assume in any moment, so that we can show up as we need to in that situation, filling just the need that is present. If we are with another person, there is something that other person needs from us. And yes, we have to be ourselves with that other person if we are to be authentic and real, if we are to embody the love that is within us. But when we are embodying love, and we are doing so masterfully in our life, we are past the point of wondering if we are going to be ourselves. We know we could not help but be ourselves.

With that assurance, then you can ask: How do I serve this person? How do I provide exactly what is needed for them? Something they could accept and receive from me, which would be of true service? I may need to be a rock for another person. There is the paradox: I have the fluidity to be that rock. I have the fluidity to show up and be the body of love that is exactly right in this circumstance.

You often hear people use the metaphor of a duck swimming across the water: oh, so graceful, with the ripples extending out beyond it. But under the water there is the rapid paddling of little webbed feet! That is a metaphor for us in showing up as love in our world and providing just the right thing. It takes internal work to be fluid enough to show up as who you need to be for another person or for a circumstance.

Sometimes it takes melting inside to allow the love that is within you to be liquid and to flow to another in just the right way. It can take internal heat to transform what has become stony inside, so that it becomes fluid. And then you offer something solid outside to the people around you. You can embody love as the stone cut out without hands.

So many people who lack true assurance confuse what is meant to be solid and what is meant to be fluid. Instead of being fluid on the inside, so that their love can take exactly the right shape in the circumstance at hand, they let themselves become hard on the inside. They think they know how other people should be, how the circumstance should be, or even how they themselves should be. They are not pouring out their love.

They are attempting to make people conform to their idea about how they should be. They are trying to create a stone cut out by the use of their hands. And it never works.

Let us build the body of love. That body is created in ways that can seem inglorious. It is a building, one step at a time, one relationship built on universal love at a time. We have to begin for it to occur. So often, so-called spiritual people are "all dressed up with no place to go." No beginning. No understanding that the body of love is built step-by-step. It is built through the discipline of embodying love in every little thing: stone on stone, brick on brick. It begins as all true things begin, as something so small it can hardly be seen, something that seems inglorious. But when you humble yourself to the discipline of the true building process, it becomes the stone cut out without hands that turns into a great mountain.

So how open are you to be just what this circumstance needs? To be as hard and as strong as this circumstance requires, as big and as power-ful, as enduring, as tenacious, as decisive as this circumstance requires, willing to say yes and willing to say no—and, at the same time, as soft and as sweet, as fluid and as loving, and as compassionate as is needed right here and now. Whatever it is, I am here for this. I am not here for me. I am not here to prove who I am. I am already me. I am here for this moment, this person, this circumstance, and to pour my love into it.

The body of love comes together because there is a reality within that body that is replicated throughout it. The Being of love, Universal Being, is being replicated throughout that body. Your Being. That reality is the core of what humanity is. It is the core of who you are. Within all seven billion of us there is one Being of love that's being replicated throughout.

Most people are largely unconscious of what is going on. But the body comes together because it is being replicated out of that one reality, out of that one Being of love that is the most real thing about who you are. Yes, there are all the individual aspects of us as human beings, and love expresses differently through each of us. There are unique colors of spirit that we each bring. But at the core of who we are, we are that one Being of love, that one focus of white light that, in the wonder of Being, is refracted into the rainbow of all light.

How have you been trying to prove who you are?
What can you do to embrace who you are without trying to prove it?

Call Down the Thunder

Transform this hallowed earth,
changed forever as
the lightning in the heaven of Being
crackles in a wet sky,
surrounding your bowed head
and furrowed brow.

Call down the thunder
that shakes the air
and rattles the windows and walls.
Through you, the voice of planets
and the light of stars
appears in the world of men,
and the fire of suns
consumes the insanity of a person
who believes they are right
while measuring nothing
and next to nothing,
to find one virtuous
and the other wrong.

Through you,
the king of all glory,
his great heart pumping
with the blood of the universe,
has now appeared.

The deed is done,
and all that is dead
dies forever
so that what is alive
may live through you,
through all,
and flourish in the world
once more.

The Party Inside You

We cannot settle for a vision of a human being that sees us as simply a hollow reed through which spirit is going to come into the world. Oh, that it were that simple! But that is not how it is for us as human beings. That might be the beginning of a process of spiritual awakening, but what we discover is that if our full potential is going to be realized, it has to come through the dynamics of our humanity, which, in fact, is made for just that.

It is tempting to attempt some kind of spiritual bypass, so that the spiritual can come into the world in a way that doesn't involve these human capacities or our relationships with other people. If only we could get the ego out of the way. Many spiritual practices are designed to let the usual self-directed sense of self move into the background to make space for a transcendent experience. That can be wonderful. But what happens when you move into all the other areas—your work life, home life, and your relationships with others?

Our fulfillment as a human being calls us to be far more than an open channel. The wisdom and power of the universe is not coming through us, leaving us untouched as it streams out to the world around us. It is throwing a wild party inside us on the way through!

A real and complete spiritual experience involves both oneness and dynamism. Universal Love brings an experience of oneness—between oneself and all Creation, among people, and with Universal Love. Dynamism requires at least two. Dynamism is created when there is a relationship between at least two things and there is power at work in that relationship.

There is dynamism between energy and matter. In the human experience, there is dynamism between the creative energy within people and the forms of their life—their thoughts, feelings, and actions. So here is a question to think about: Does the universal energy and consciousness come to you as one integrated reality? Does all of it relate to all of you?

Or is it more complicated than that? Maybe parts of that one reality come into parts of you and then interact. Maybe that is what it is like to be a human being.

Certainly, between us as people, energy and consciousness are both streaming through us all together all the time and also interacting among us. Universal consciousness may activate my thoughts that I express to you, which then activate your expression of Universal Love through your emotions. Your emotional expression of Universal Love might activate someone else's actions, which are born from universal consciousness and Universal Love.

The divine masculine can express through a man, and that expression can interact with the divine feminine through a woman. In that case, divine masculine and divine feminine have not yet had the union they will know through that man and woman prior to having been expressed through them. They are in dynamic relationship in human form, and their union is fulfilled in form if they let it be.

So it is clear that there is spiritual dynamism taking place among us as human beings. While it takes an uncommon personal perspective to see it, the same thing is happening within people all the time. Masculine and feminine dynamics are constantly at work. Thought is affecting emotion and emotion is affecting thought. And when people are open to the spirit of love within them, it is affecting both thought and feeling. All of this motivates the overt physical action of the individual.

It seems so easy to think of all that happens in us and among us as human beings as if it were just a human experience. It isn't! It is the Divine at work dynamically through the human experience. Usually, it gets messy because the people involved have so little consciousness of what is happening. The opportunity for divine dynamism turns into human drama.

So here's my point. There are all-powerful universal forces at work inside you all the time, and you could let that happen in a totally masterful way. Those forces are interacting with one another and that is what is bringing dynamism to your experience. Think of it! The truth of the universe is constantly activating your thoughts. You might not be open to it, but it's trying. The love of the universe is constantly working in your emotional realm. That's why being human is such a wild ride.

This image of an ancient cross is from the island of Rhodes in Greece. Its date of origin is 585 BC.

The symbol shows the four cosmic forces, symbolized by the four arms of this cross, all of which are in motion. This symbolizes the constantly changing dynamism within all Creation and within us as human beings. So even if people think they have life figured out for a moment, the dynamic changes.

While this can seem mystical and esoteric, it is, at the same time, immediate and familiar. Because these four cosmic forces appear through these four aspects of a human being: thoughts, feelings, the physical body, and the human spirit. They are all an expression of the Godhead, the Creator, the source of all Creation meeting within you, to join in you and become the expression of you to the world. That's dynamism!

Jesus spoke brilliantly about the way this process works. Addressing the human experience, in Mark 12:30, KJB, he said this:

Thou shalt love the Lord thy God with all thy heart, and with all thy soul, and with all thy mind, and with all thy strength: this is the first commandment.

Jesus is speaking about four aspects of human experience.

Heart = Feeling

Soul = Human Spirit

Mind = Thought

Strength = Physical Body

The four cosmic forces at work through these four aspects of the human experience move into an elegant dynamic relationship, without a "grinding of gears" when the human experience is acknowledged by the human being as originating in the Creator and when the human capacity is in total love response to the source of the energy that is coming through it. And when you exercise your courage to embrace your own humanity as those four cosmic forces move through you, your courage creates the gravity that holds you together. Then the dynamism has the opportunity to come into the rhythm of the Creator, represented by the ancient symbol on the previous page. There is elegance, grace, wholesomeness, and vitality in the creative process.

The Creator is throwing a party inside you. Enjoy it! Invite others to join the celebration!

What can you do to not miss out on the party
the Creator is throwing in you and for you?

Pleasure and Fulfillment

Imagine for a moment that you were the creator of the universe. What possible reason could you have had for creating it? Imagine living somewhere in the realm of the infinite and the eternal, thinking about the possibility of creating stars, nebula, dark matter, and light. Think about creating Planet Earth with forests and seas, beasts of all kinds, and even people.

What reason could there be for creating it all, other than your own pleasure and fulfillment? The pleasure of the creative process and the fulfillment of embodying something wonderful in living form. What joy unspeakable to create a universe singing with your cosmic energy! What pleasure to create a world on this planet, with a biosphere that sustains so many remarkable species of life! And what fulfillment to be able to incarnate in the space-time continuum as a human being!

In the story of the Seven Days of Creation, in Genesis 1:31, KJB, it says, "And God saw every thing that he had made, and behold, *it was* very good." When the Creation was complete the verse says, "Behold, *it was* very good." This was God taking pleasure in Creation.

Pleasure and fulfillment are part of the experience of self. Can you imagine a real self who could not have these experiences? A person who could not experience pleasure and fulfillment would be more like an automaton or a slave than a real human being. The signers of the Declaration of Independence of the 13 original United States of America had this in mind when they spoke about the right to the "pursuit of Happiness."

But it is hard to think about pleasure and fulfillment without reflecting on all the trouble people get into because of their search for those experiences. It can lead to terrible addictions and substance abuse. It can lead a person to act destructively toward other people and to the world. As a species, our unconscious search for pleasure and fulfillment is threatening our existence through global warming and nuclear war.

So what is the difference between a life-giving experience of pleasure and fulfillment and an experience of addiction and self-destruction? That's an important distinction for anyone to figure out in their life!

It really comes down to this. Generosity is the source of all virtue. As you are connected to the generosity of all Being that dwells within you, you are nourished from within. The generosity at your core feeds all the rest of you. It emanates from you. There is pleasure in that emanation. As Olympic racer Eric Liddell wrote in *The Disciplines of the Christian Life*, later told in the movie *Chariots of Fire*, "When I run, I feel His pleasure." The human soul knows pleasure as the love and wisdom of Being pours through it.

Nourished from within, you can appreciate that the cycles of creation are *already* bringing you what is rightfully yours. They are *already* giving you what you need. It might not be all of what you need right now. But when you take pleasure in what is now coming to you, when you enjoy it with gratitude and appreciation, you are being yourself. You are being a creator. You are acting like a creator. You are setting yourself up to experience a greater fulfillment in your life in the days to come.

The alternative isn't good. Grabbing at things that are not really yours—that are not coming to you in the cycles of creation—is a violation of your own Being and a violation of the creation. Believing you do not have enough pleasure, and then attempting to create it in artificial ways, does not satisfy. It does not bring fulfillment. It does not bring life. Addiction does not make people happy. Neither does getting what you think you want when it does not really belong to you.

Ultimately, what anyone else thinks about you in this regard is unimportant next to the truth of the matter. And you are the one who can learn to discern what that truth is—what is rightly yours and what is coming to you in the cycles of creation. You will probably make mistakes along the way. Most people do.

But as you stay in generosity and gratitude, you will learn to let the world come to you and give you pleasure. And joy. And fulfillment. After all, the Being who you are is the creator of your world. So if you let the cycles of creation move in their own true rhythm, the day will come when you can look at your creation and say, "It is good."

What can you take pleasure in right now?
What is good?

Your Little Town

Step through the oak casement
onto the main thoroughfare of your little town.
Greet the sunlight warming your cheeks
and shining off last night's snow
that lies in rainbows at the sidewalk's edge.
This is your day!
This frigid air is for you!
These people passing by are your people
looking in the hidden corner of their heart for you and your blessing.
Step into your town!
Greet your world!
Welcome this day!

All-In

This quotation is from Theodore Roosevelt, 1906 Nobel Peace Prize recipient, leader of the "Rough Riders" First US Volunteer Cavalry in the Spanish–American War, conservationist, and 26th president of the United States. It's excerpted from a 1910 speech, titled "Citizenship in a Republic":

> It is not the critic who counts; not the man who points out how the strong man stumbles, or where the doer of deeds could have done them better. The credit belongs to the man who is actually in the arena, whose face is marred by dust and sweat and blood; who strives valiantly; who errs, who comes up short again and again, because there is no effort without error and shortcoming; but who does actually strive to do the deeds; who knows great enthusiasms, the great devotions; who spends himself in a worthy cause; who at the best knows in the end the triumph of high achievement, and who at the worst, if he fails, at least fails while daring greatly, so that his place shall never be with those cold and timid souls who neither know victory nor defeat.

These words encourage anyone who reads them to be "all-in" in their life. Being all-in doesn't necessarily mean that you are on horseback, saber brandished high. Being all-in means totally owning and being totally engaged in what is happening in your life. And when I say "engaged," I don't mean all enmeshed. I just mean that you are fully present, fully here.

There is no way to unthink a thought or unfeel a feeling or undo what has been done. You can't unsee what you have seen. The crucial factor is whether you are seeing from the standpoint of someone who is fully engaged in life—someone who is all-in. That is related to the vantage point from which you observe and how you relate to what we see.

In Teddy Roosevelt's time, as in our own, the tendency to stand on the sidelines of our own life as the distant critic is epidemic. The critic attributes the cause of things to other people and applauds or criticizes from a distance. In the media, this is a popular sport. Personally, I seldom enjoy movies the film critics praise. And I've always had a secret desire to become a movie-critic critic—to write a column critiquing other people's movie reviews. But really that has only passing interest, because being all-in, in my own life, is too important to me.

The point is that when you fully own your life, something kicks in that cannot kick in any other way. There are forces and energies and there is wisdom that kicks in when you are 100 percent "in" that doesn't kick in at 99 percent. So it is more than the courage and valor, which is so much a part of Teddy Roosevelt's spirit, that kicks in. I'm all for courage and valor, but there's more to life than that. There is wisdom that kicks in; patience and endurance that kick in. There is sight that kicks in when *you* are *all*-in.

Being all-in in your life does mean giving all of who you are. As it's said in sports, it is "leaving it all on the field." But this is not about burnout, because if you are fully committed to your life, you can't afford burnout. You are not here for burnout. You are in for the long haul. If you are fully committed to the creative process that we are in the midst of, however it is manifesting, you are there to enjoy the fulfillment of the cycle. That is something different from the short burst, making a good show of it, looking valiant in one moment and then passing out from exhaustion.

Really owning your life is owning its fulfillment and being committed to doing your part in whatever phase of the cycle you are in. If you are bursting with action, all-in looks like tasks, movement, and productivity. If you are in the atmosphere of understanding, all-in looks like paying attention to and adjusting perspectives and the dynamics of your thoughts, feelings, and behaviors. If you are enjoying the rays of enlightenment, all-in might look like solitude. Whatever phase of the creative process you are in . . . be ALL-IN.

What does it mean to be all-in in relationship? It includes the ability to protect the heart of another person. Our human anatomy tells us a lot about this. We have a physical heart, perhaps the most vital organ in our body. It is closely connected to our emotional body. Notice where the heart is. Some people are said to wear their heart on their sleeves, but of course that is not actually true in a physical sense. Your heart is in a special place, surrounded by your rib cage and your breastbone. It is in a protected place, as well it should be.

This demonstrates something that ought to be true for us as human beings—that our own emotional realm is in a protected place. It is a good place to be, where it's not necessarily subject to every passing thing. It has a place to be that is protected, where the tender essences of the heart can thrive, and therefore deepen and vitalize our own life and the lives of other people.

Can you be the breastbone or the rib cage for the emotional realm of another person, so that you are keeping safe what's happening there for him or her? The delicate flow of his or her heart is being protected by your strength. You are keeping out the impact of words and energy that could make it difficult for his or her emotional realm to be at peace. Sometimes we are called on to be the protection of the heart when there are soft and delicate essences that are growing there. Realities that need to emerge through the heart need a place to grow, away from the harsh things of the everyday world.

This is about being a warrior of the heart—a warrior for the protection of the gentle things that can grow there. When a person performs that function for themselves or another person, the heart has many gifts to give back. One such gift is warmth and encouragement. The protected heart has that to give to us as we are about the work that is ours to do in the world. The protected heart energizes us to truly be all-in. It is hard to have the courage of a Teddy Roosevelt if your own passionate heart is not behind your presence in the world. To be all-in, your heart needs to be behind you and encouraging you. And for that to happen, you must be its protection, its breastbone and rib cage.

These dynamics can play out creatively between people. In conventional society, the man has been the warrior in the world and comes home to protect the woman from the perils of the world at large. There can be something beautiful about a dynamic between a man and a woman, in which the man protects the heart of the woman and the soft and gentle things that can be born through that heart, and where the woman offers her encouragement and support for the man's work in the world. If he can't offer that kind of protection, she might never find a protected place for the gentleness of her heart to emerge. Or at least he'll never get to see it. But if, in that scenario, there is protection for the heart of a woman, she has the opportunity to be an encourager, to say, "I'm with you, I'm behind you—you have my heart."

This dynamic can be at play regardless of gender—among women, among men, and between men and women. When it is, reciprocity is beginning to occur. The heart of one person reciprocates by offering encouragement when it receives the protection of another. When receiving encouragement, a person can reciprocate by protecting the heart of the one who encourages.

Full reciprocity takes people beyond an experience of fixed roles. It carries a person into an experience of taking the role that another person has been in. For example, the man who has been protecting the heart of a woman finds that she is then protecting his. And the woman who has been giving the warmth and enthusiasm of her heart to a man then finds that he is giving his warmth and enthusiastic heart to her. If someone has protected your heart, aren't you inspired to protect theirs, to be a champion for them, to make a safe place for their heart to open up?

This is part of what it means to be all-in. When it comes to relationship, being all-in doesn't necessarily mean that you have a lifelong commitment. It means that you are fully present and committed to whatever kind of relationship this is meant to be. It might be a life partner; it might be a business partner. It might be a friend or a brother or a sister. Being all-in changes any relationship.

These words from David Whyte's poem "The Truelove" speak of being all-in, in relationship.

There is a faith in loving fiercely
the one who is rightfully yours . . . .

Part of *loving fiercely* is protecting the sacred things of the heart that are present for other people. Those sacred things need a home in which they can grow and flourish.

So who is the one that is rightfully yours? It is whoever is in your life right now. Life is best lived all-in.

What will you do to be all-in in your life and your relationships?

The Other Side of the World

He thought there might be adventure
on the other side of the world,
past the silly stone pillars
of the cul-de-sac
and out beyond the well-edged lawns
that made his mind ache
and his soul grieve
as he drove by.

He dreamed of a wild land
where his mother was once born
and beasts still roamed,
stalking their prey.
His heart could mend in such a place,
hearing the liquid call of larks at dawn,
and watching the sun as it climbed across the sky.

If he stared long enough into the evening prayer fires,
sang to the pines and mosses and ferns,
and worshipped with the herons and hawks
at the edge of the mountain pond,
the sickness of his spirit would heal,

and he would remember again
who he was,
where he came from,
and what he must do next.

Yes, there would be adventure
on the other side of the world,
and a chance to know himself again as he was
outside of this little place
where he had been living;
a chance to set himself free.

Spiritual and Emotional Mastery

Even though there is the appearance that you and all the other people around the world are leading separate lives, the truth is that we are connected to all people around the world. There is one body of consciousness for humanity, even though we each have our own piece of it.

What we think and what we feel, and what moves in our spirit, are connected to what people think and feel and have happen for them spiritually all around the world. It didn't take the mass media or the Internet to make that so, although sometimes these technologies remind us of what is already true, and facilitate the experience that there is one body of consciousness for all of humanity.

Some people in this world are called to play a special role of positive influence in human consciousness. In the world that we live in, influence is usually associated with money. And the media has power to influence people, whether it's the television or the print media or the Internet. But the ultimate power of influence is built into the nature of humanity and the nature of consciousness. Because, even though it seems like consciousness is separate, and you've got yours and I've got mine, we are all dipping into the same pool. All people are connected around the world. So what happens in my consciousness influences you, and what happens for you influences me.

In fact, there's a shape to consciousness. There are layers of consciousness that function like a pyramid. And what happens at higher and higher levels tends to influence what happens below, and what happens at the apex of consciousness affects everything else in that pyramid. That's certainly true for us individually. It's said that if you want to have the maximum influence in someone's life, change their relationship to God. Why? It is because that relationship takes place in this apex point of consciousness. If what is present at that apex point changes, it affects the rest of the body of consciousness.

How you relate to the unseen is a critical factor in your life—what you believe about God, what you understand God to be, shapes your human experience. If you live with an angry, vengeful God, you're likely to live an angry, vengeful life. If you understand that God is a God of love, that the universe is a universe of love, and that the intent for your life and mine is born out of love, that changes your life.

The word we use for people who are called to that apex place in consciousness for humanity is *priesthood*. There are men and women who don't necessarily know each other, around the world, who hear the call to play their part in that priesthood. They are probably not wearing special clothing, and they are not taking certain religious vows. But the issues that are configuring in their lives and in their thoughts and feelings relate to their calling. They are called to let what is present at the apex of the whole body of human consciousness change.

These men and women are called to spiritual mastery, by whatever name. They are called to be spiritual masters, not out of arrogance or of pretense, not out of human whim or determination. They are called to be masterful in letting what's present in the invisible pour through and transform consciousness. And if we are called in this way, it really doesn't matter much that there are many other people who do not hear the same call. We have the work that is ours to do.

So there is a need and a call to the spiritual maturity that is necessary for spiritual mastery. What I've found is there's no such thing as spiritual mastery or spiritual maturity without first there being emotional maturity and emotional mastery. No matter how accurate what a person believes might be, it is of no consequence if there is no emotional maturity and emotional mastery. Because people can believe what they will, even the truest belief and the truest intention can come undone in the application. This is true in any area of life. But it is particularly so when it comes to spiritual mastery.

I have friends who object to the term *emotional mastery*. I think it's because it evokes the idea that we're going to mentally control our emotions. Have you ever succeeded in controlling your emotions through mental willpower? I doubt it. You might be a master of repression, but usually that only works for so long. As human beings are out of touch with the spiritual reality within them, they cannot master their emotions.

Emotional mastery takes emotional surrender. It implies being mastered by what you're surrendering to. And the only way that real emotional mastery comes is as the emotional body surrenders to the unseen.

When it comes to physical things, you can draw concise and accurate diagrams of what it is you are describing. When it comes to building a house, you can draw up the architectural plans and get the carpenter and plumber and everybody else to follow the plans. When it comes to spiritual things, it's not so easy. We can draw diagrams, but the diagrams are diagramming something that is unseen. We can use metaphors and parables and symbols and stories to say something about the unseen; we can give it names. But people have to find it for themselves.

And the only way to find it fully is through surrender. It takes courage to surrender. And your surrender brings the gravity of who you are. There is no other way. No one ever masters spirit. If there is mastery, it is because you surrender and let what is in the unseen master you. Never is that more true than when it comes to emotions. While the mind has a part to play in emotional mastery, it's not because the mind is going to master the emotions.

On the outer edge of the emotional body, there are four primary human emotions: fear, anger, happiness, and sadness. These four emotions relate to the longing of the human soul. A key factor is whether there is a conscious openness to the influence of spirit that lets in what the soul is longing for.

The human soul cries out for a fuller experience of the unseen spirit that is its source. And when it cries out, it seems like it's crying out in anger and in sadness and in fear, and in happiness. When spiritual reality is present and available through a person and the emotions are opened up to that reality, the spiritual reality has the opportunity to answer the call of the emotional body, to step in and give the emotional body what it's looking for—to say, in essence, "I know what you want." When the spiritual reality of a person steps into that emotional body, the experience changes.

Most people are afraid of their own emotions and, for the most part, do their best to sideline them so they don't interfere with their life. They feel threatened by their emotions, much as a parent might feel threatened by a crying, angry child. We have the opportunity to hear the calls of the emotional body and to step in and to bring the authority of spirit. And, from the standpoint of our emotional body, we have a chance to release and be mastered by the reality of spirit, which is our own ultimate reality.

So I'll tell you what I think people are crying out for when they're angry. I think they're crying to find their own strength as individuals. They're crying out to find their own life force. They're looking for that and having a hard time finding it. When, in immaturity, somebody cries out for their own strength, it comes out as anger. And when the fullness of their spirit comes into their emotional body, it brings strength and centeredness, and it brings life, which is what the person was asking for. You can try it out yourself, when you feel what seems to you to be anger rising up in you. If your spirit steps into that and lets the current of spirit move in and through your emotional body, if you let your strength be present, you'll find that the call of your soul is answered.

Sadness, or grief, is another emotion that people often avoid. If you step into that emotion, you will find there is the longing for the internal flow that brings connection, ultimately the longing for connection with spirit itself, a connection with love. That is the longing of the soul. What I find is that my sadness and grief won't kill me. People might think it will—that they will drown in it forever. If you fully step into it with your spirit, you'll find out what your soul is longing for. And on the other side of what seems to be sadness, there is the connection, union, and oneness.

What is the soul looking for when it experiences fear? It is seeking awareness. Not just a knowing of the immediate facts but intelligence that sees current reality from a higher perspective.

What is the ultimate awareness? It is that the highest reality of who I am is not this person who seems to be the victim of circumstance. It's the knowing that I am the creator of my world; I am the one who holds the creative process of my world. I am not what's being created; I am not what is disintegrating and breaking down in the creative process. I am the one who is holding all of that with my gravity. I am the creator of my world.

For people who have had a chance to face their own death, they have had a grand opportunity to know what's on the other side of fear, which is that I am not what I've created—I am what created it. That brings a certain fearlessness in being in the world, if you know that about yourself. Moving through your own fear, there is what's on the other side, which is altitude and perspective and the ability to hold the creative process. I don't see how people do that if they're totally embedded in their successes and their failures, or with all the little births and deaths of their life—and there are plenty of them. On the other side of fear is the perspective that *I hold it all.*

On the other side of happiness, and the desire to be happy, is love—Love with a big *L*, the ultimate of human experience. We find out that our love is boundless; it knows no end. Love is no respecter of persons. And while it might seem hard to try to love people you don't like, on the other side of happiness is the experience that you really can't help loving everybody. That doesn't mean that there aren't distances among people in the outer flow of our life. But the biggest part of us is like that. We bring Divine Love.

So we are called to emotional maturity, not emotional repression or emotional recklessness. Where there is emotional maturity and emotional mastery, who and what we are can vibrate with spirit, and we are in position to have a profound influence in the body of the consciousness of humanity. For one thing, we are generating the substance of consciousness at the highest level. We're filling in what's been missing, which is real connection to the invisible.

This is what it really takes for there to be an experience of the invisible. As the poet Hafiz said in "Tired of Speaking Sweetly," when that really starts happening,

> *Most everyone I know*
> *Quickly packs their bags and hightails it*
> *Out of town.*

It's one thing to think about it, but what if you ask people to let something change in their emotional body? My experience is that the response often is, "Anything but that!" People who seek spiritual mastery have to turn that around and deliberately do something about the openness and clarity of their emotional experience.

The substance of the emotional body determines what happens in your life and in mine, and in the life of humanity. Do you think the advertisers of the world want that from you? The advertisers of the world want your emotional body, make no mistake. The politicians of the world want your emotional body. The businesspeople of the world and the financiers of the world want your emotional body. The religious leaders of the world want your emotional body. And for most people, they've all got it. Because if they've got your feelings, they've got your money, they've got your labor, they've got your thinking, and they've got your way of living. They've got you.

So the gold standard for setting the direction of a person's life, and the life of humanity, is the ability to capture the response of the emotional body.

> *As a man thinketh in his heart, so is he.*
> *~ Proverbs 23:7, KJB ~*

That is where he will go. If we find ourselves working with what is at the apex of consciousness, we are interested in letting the emotional body be set free so that spiritual reality can govern in human consciousness, and so that the reality of who we are as Divine Beings can be present in and through human consciousness. As we let it be so for ourselves, the capstone experience is present for us personally and for humankind.

Where are you being ruled by your emotions?
Which people or groups of people are holding the strings?

A Spring Prayer

I say to you again that the winter is gone,

And the patch of snow in the furl near the pasture

Is all that's left of her white cloak.

The creek by our farmhouse is filled with the melt of spring,

And the robins who flew south not to face the fierce winter winds

Are even now hunting earthworms in this morning's sun.

O Love, have our hearts weathered the cold of a winter past?

Or did they turn frigid and brittle with the icicles

that hung off the eves after Christmas?

Too hard to notice the purple crocus has already blossomed.

The elk have come down out of the mountains

Because it is in our fields where the grass has first turned green,

Our valley where they find this spring's food.

Come now out of the house,

Love of my heart,

And see how they graze!

Let our home exhale the stale air from our winter fires

And breathe in this good spring breeze

Which wafts in from the prairies.

Please, O love, come out of the house,

While the day is still long,

So that we may walk together among the hills,

Laugh over what has been,

And celebrate the promise which this new day brings.

Yes, O love, the winter is gone.

And our hearts melt now in the noonday sun,

To celebrate this new life carried in your womb,

And to praise what may be born between us,

To grow in the warmth of summer's sun.

The day is still long.

May our hearts wend their way to one another,

So that we may share the unfolding glory of this life together.

Chapter Seven

THE RADIANCE AND REFLECTIONS

OF

GRACE

As you dissolve into love, your ego fades. You're not thinking about loving; you're just being love, radiating like the sun.

~ RAM DASS ~

Grace

Your destiny is to become a sun. You are already a sun on the inside. You are becoming a sun on the outside. Right in the middle of your human experience. In the middle of all that is living, growing, and rising, and all that is tragic, broken, wounded, or dying, you are becoming a sun.

There is so much you do not know about why the world is the way it is, or why human beings are the way they are. There is so much about the path of life that you cannot see. But deep within you, you know that you are becoming a sun—a profound expression of love that is so large, so all-consuming, that you can scarcely entertain the thought.

Your life path has been leading you to this knowing—all the inspiration, all the struggle, all the openness, all the aspiration, all the love you have known in your life, and all the grief and disappointment. All that you have accomplished and all your failures have led you to this moment of deep knowing—that you are becoming a sun in the middle of it all.

This is the grace that has always been present in your human experience. It contains the knowing that both the wonder of creation and the terror of it reveal something so magnificent, so glorious, that words can hardly tell. And you can appreciate that you would never come to this knowing without having committed yourself to your very human experience. You could not have become such a human being of love any other way. There was no other way for you to become a sun. There is no other way for anyone to become a sun.

Because you are a sun, you can embrace the incompleteness of your humanity. And you can embrace the incompleteness of others. Because you are a sun, you have a profound forgiveness for the ugliness of what is present within people and within yourself. And profound appreciation that right there within what is incomplete in people is the radiance of the sun. Whether or not they know it, they are becoming a sun too.

You know that you have been playing your part in the unfoldment of creation. But it is clear that there is a larger order in which it is all held and to which it all returns. It is enough that you are shining your light. You are bringing the warmth of your sun to the world. You are bringing your gravity. And the universe is so grateful that you are doing your part in your appointed place. The universe has always wanted this for you.

Thank you for becoming a sun.

Where in your life are you being the sun?

My Beloved Fills Her Straw Basket

My beloved fills her straw basket
With the pears and apples of this Indian summer,
And lifts them high on the shelf in the kitchen
To be kissed by the autumnal sun
Shining over the red café curtains.
Her body stretched to the limits of her earthly frame,
She slides her bounty beside the green tomatoes
And the velvet Concord grapes
Ripening in the late-afternoon light.

O, that all her days
Could be filled with this glory!
For her to taste each ripe fruit
With her hungry, flashing eyes
As she lays one beside another.

If only her every harvest
Could be this sweet,
This crisp,
This full of July sun!
What I would do
To see that day!

So I watch her now,

Hoping to prolong this golden moment with one adoring gaze,

And paint all her life

With today's yellow light.

And I pray her December snows and springtime rains

Are filled with the love

She lifts in her basket,

In the luscious white flesh

Of the harvest she raises high

On this warm October afternoon.

Do you believe you have the capacity to bring a profound, positive impact to another person's life? I believe that we each have the ability to bring the grace of God to another person. An encounter with the grace of God is always life-changing.

In the presence of that grace, our whole makeup reshapes and reforms. And while the grace of God is always present, when it is embodied through a person, it makes a profound difference for all the people who are in touch with that grace through them.

How have you encountered grace in your life?
How could you offer it to others?

The Grace of the Great Mother

I have a friend who lives in Littleton, Colorado. Her name is Jennifer Deisher and she has a blog under the name *The Moon Hippie Mystic*. This is from her 2014 blog post "Grow the Garden" (see https://blueprintsforbutterflies.com/). She speaks of Mother Gaia, the feminine face of God.

> *She is waiting for you. She has a secret for you if you Listen. Grow my garden.*
>
> *Come to me, I'm Always here and I'm Always free . . .*
>
> *The most Beautiful things grow from the deepest, darkest places. Dig deep into the mud. Dig the hole. Plant the seed. Give me your shame and we will plant a seed of Compassion. Tell me your secrets along the rambling river. Show me resentment and I will show you how to grow Forgiveness. Feel my Light coming through the trees. Let me show you where to plant denial so you will blossom with Truth and Light.*
>
> *Climb my mountain. Let me feel where you are weary and you will see how you have Persevered.*

These beautiful words embody the grace of the Great Mother. They are words of spirit and yet they are words of Jennifer Deisher, Moon Hippie Mystic. They are words that were uttered through a person who found a way to crack open enough to allow the spirit of the Great Mother to speak through her.

We all have that same opportunity—to crack wide open so that the Great Mother can be present through our presence. The mystery and wonder of the Mother of All can be with other people because we are with other people and we have cracked open and we let it be so. There might be words to say to give voice to that wonder and the mystery. But ultimately it is our presence in a state of having been cracked open, so that our humanity is transforming and bringing the presence of the grace of God.

You might be able to guess, from hearing Jennifer's words, that this is not a woman who has lived a conventional life, who has just tiptoed down the path of life in joy and peace and all good things, with no challenges and no adventures on that path. She speaks from her own experience of having been cracked wide open. We do not bring the grace of God because we park our humanity someplace else and become a channel for God's grace. It is because we have come face-to-face with the grace of God ourselves, in the middle of the calamity of the human experience, that we have that grace to bring to other people.

In the face of our humanity, in the face of whatever challenges there are in our own life, in the face of our anxiety, our sense of victimhood, our own denial, frustrations, we have allowed the grace of God to come into us and transform it all. We have been willing to give it all up to the Great Mother.

Jennifer's blog continues with these words:

When you find lack I will sprout in you the seed of Gratitude . . . Open me to your fear and I will teach you Courage of the Heart . . . Dig deeply and plant the seed of ignorance so I may enlighten you with my Diversity . . . Plant the seed of unworthiness and I will show you the Love that you are . . .

Unburden to me your addictions and I will bring you Freedom on the wings of Angels.

We each have the potential within us to be that one who brings this message of the Great Mother. We might use words to bring it. But beyond words, somehow, at some unseen level of communication among us as human beings, you know if this grace is present in me, and I know if it is present and available from you. The presence of grace is filled with safety and love and forgiveness and renewal. There is rebirth that is possible in that presence. All old things can be left behind.

Through that presence there is intercession, meaning that the grace of God has the possibility of interceding in another person's life and changing it, of saying, "I don't care what's happened up to now; I don't care what trajectory your life seemed to be on. It's now changing to something wonderful in my presence."

What I notice is that when the grace of God is present through a person, those around them recalculate their lives. They sort their lives out in a different way. Perhaps they have been trying to sort it out in desperation, in a way where there did not seem to be any possibility. But now they are seeing possibility where there was none. They are seeing options where it looked like there were no options. And they are finding all those experiences that the spirit of love brings to a person—the feeling of self-worth, real meaning, value, and the lifting of the awful burden of shame with which so many people live. The grace of the Great Mother says, "Come to me, I'm always here, and I'm always free."

It moves me deeply that Jennifer had a confrontation with grace in her own life, and that it interceded so profoundly for her that she cannot help but share what she experienced. That is how it is for people when they have experienced something life-changing. Their gratitude for that awakens in them a profound reciprocity, a profound desire to give back and to pay it forward.

It is possible, in that process, to become world-weary and to come to the belief that nobody really wants your gift anyway, and that maybe what you have experienced yourself and what was so important to you is not really important to other people. And, after all, it's been ignored by some and perhaps even ridiculed by others. So people decide to keep it to themselves.

I am inviting you to this: If God's grace has changed your life, recall the difference that that made for you. And live this day and every day of your life, from this day forward, with that passion. Give what you were given, with the same gratitude and the same joy with which you received it, to every person you meet. Make it available, without imposition. Act on that passion every day of your life, and embody it in your presence in the simplest of your interactions with other people.

Because what makes the difference in this world is the presence of that grace, fully embodied in a person. So whatever you are about, and whatever the challenges and the ups and downs of a given day or week or year might happen to be within that, welcome the grace of God. Make it possible for others to feel and even begin to reflect the grace you are radiating.

It is that grace that makes the difference in our world, because in it is the template of a whole person. Each one of us came to Earth to be a living embodiment of that template, and that is not only what is the salvation of every person we meet but it is the salvation of our world— that template through humanity.

A whole person creates whole community—whatever community you are a part of. A whole person who is bringing that template is showing that template to the community and saying, "As a community we could be like this. We could be whole. We could be embodying this template and expressing this wholeness to the world."

It is our destiny, each one of us, to bring that template to our community, to our family, to our friends, to our loved ones, to whatever organization we might be participating in, so that the community of whatever size and whatever nature could itself be a living template of wholeness for the world. That is the great calling and the great need of this day. That is God's grace at work in the world.

How have you been cracked open?
How has grace changed your life?
How could it change the lives of those around you and
be reflected into the world?

The Sacred Valley

This reading is a vision for the future that I had several years ago of the home where I live at Sunrise Ranch. It is a vision of a healing between the inner nature of humanity and our manifest experience. The vision is becoming real for us here in many ways. I read these words in 2013 at the first annual Arise Festival at Sunrise Ranch. The words were a prophecy come true for the people who were attending the festival. But the vision is not really just for Sunrise Ranch. The Sacred Valley is a metaphor for Planet Earth and all Her people.

The Sacred Valley

Into that sacred valley, in that day, the people of the world came, family after family, company after company, to find the healing vibration that rung in the air between the pine-covered hills and the red sandstone rock. Through what they experienced there, each found their own wholeness, and their own place in the family of man. And each found their own unique and private relationship with the king and queen of this magical land.

Those who greeted and hosted all who came shared in sacred, daily ritual themselves, in right relationship with the land, and the inhabitants of all the kingdoms of the valley. They danced by their sacred fires. They sang and played pipes and horns and drums in the amphitheatre among the granite rocks. They worshipped in the holy temple. Most of all, they loved one another, and each one came to any other among them to serve them when they were in need.

Those who visited the sacred valley left their gifts. For some silver, some gold. For some, they left their songs.

It was in those days that the earth and her peoples were healed. Old hurts were cast off. Life-threatening ways of being on the earth and with other people were dissolved, along with the lies behind them.

307

A new way, in harmony with all that is, was found. Few knew that the radiance of this sacred, little valley had shown the way. But the people of the valley didn't care. They knew what they had done.

This Golden, Shining Moment

To you who read these words, together we have this golden, shining moment in time to bring a shift in the outworking human destiny. Despite whatever sense of disillusionment might have been present for you, despite whatever failures you might believe to have been present in your own life or in our collective endeavors, this opportunity is present with us now. Knowing that consciousness is the pivotal factor for humanity and for our beloved Planet Earth, let us bring the highest reality of which we are aware to our world.

What must we do to let this happen? Most essentially, we must simply say that it shall be so. Let the highest reality come through my consciousness and yours, and let it be extended to the world. Let that reality come through our collective consciousness. With that willingness and commitment in the living of our lives, IT SHALL BE SO.

Having made this declaration, these opportunities are open to us:

- A full opening of heart and mind to the One Spirit
- A joining together in passion for our destiny to bring the transforming power of the One Spirit to the world
- Initiation of others into a knowing of the highest reality available to them

How do I know that what I speak is true? I speak from the great legacy of all the men and women who have walked this planet, bringing the spiritual victory that has brought us to this opportunity. They have done their work so that we may do ours.

I speak for many around the world who hold a creative field of consciousness through which the One Spirit has a gateway into this world. I speak from the highest reality I know and serve. Now is a critical time for Planet Earth. I do not know how long this moment will last. Let us rise to answer the opportunity before us.

The questions in my heart are these:

What can we do to answer the call of this day?
And what will we do?

Ascend the Steps of Home

Holy, holy, holy Lord.
Holy, holy, holy Lord.
We ascend the steps of home.
We come before thy sacred throne.
Standing in thy holy place,
We approach thee face to face.

Holy, holy, holy Lord.
Holy, holy, holy Lord.
Honor, glory, flows to thee!
Prince of peace,
King of love,
O Lord of hosts!

Holy, holy, holy Lord
We ascend the steps of home,
We come before thy sacred throne.
Standing in thy holy place
We see thee face to face.
We adore thee,
Come before thee,
To know thee face to face.

The Universal Field of Consciousness

The evolution of human consciousness has been taking place over millennia. That might create a picture in the mind of a slow, plodding, incremental change, bit by bit. Evolution might be seen as something that is happening *to* us, not something that's happening in and through us. But when it comes to changes in consciousness, that is not really how it happens. That is probably not how it has happened for you individually in your life, and it is not how it's happened for humanity.

The evolution of human consciousness occurs when there is a new paradigm ushered in and nurtured behind the old paradigm that seems to work. The energy of the new backs up behind that old paradigm that acts like a dam. The energy keeps growing and growing, and for a long time there are few external evidences that change is under way. But the energy keeps backing up behind the dam, and soon there are breakthroughs.

As a result, there are individual people who are pioneers in consciousness, because it does not all happen at once to all of humanity, even though the paradigm shift relates to everybody. There are people who begin to have a radically different awareness of what's happening—a radically different view of what their life is about and a radically different view of the world. They are especially open to the new paradigm, and their resistance to it is less. So the energy and the awareness of the new begin to seep through.

It's likely that people on the edge of the shift look to the world around them and ask, "Why isn't everybody else thinking and feeling what I'm thinking and feeling?" So people look for validation that what they are experiencing is real and important, and they seek that validation from other people. For the most part, they don't find it. So there is a great temptation to blend in with the crowd—a great tendency to think, "Maybe I'll just lead a so-called normal life."

It takes courage for a person to stop seeking validation from the so-called "normalcy" of the world in which they live—which is really not normal, just familiar. A spiritual pioneer learns to find validation from the already-existing field of universal consciousness. That field is always present, and it is always available. It is a field of possibility and potentiality. It is a field of what could happen in our life and in the world, if we let it. It is a world of preform. It is that universal field of consciousness that is bringing pressure on the old paradigm.

As time passes, the water keeps backing up behind the dam, and for those who are more open to that, and in whom the resistance is low enough, the water behind the dam breaks through. At that point, there begins to be a great leap forward. The dam bursts, and universal consciousness has become human consciousness.

When a person embraces the universal field of consciousness, they begin to have a radically different view of the world. From the usual perspective of spiritual or religious people, they are looking to the universal field of consciousness. They are looking to God, by whatever name. For a person who has been enmeshed in the circumstances and people of their life, opening up to the universal field of consciousness is helpful.

But something strange begins to happen to people as that opening continues. They begin to see the world through the eyes of universal consciousness. They stop seeing the world from the bottom, looking up, and begin to see the world from up, looking down. And the world looks different from that perspective. It is quite a shift to realize that you are not a struggling person who is making his or her way in life. You are universal consciousness that's looking to express itself through this sometimes resistant human being.

That looks different. It is normal but not familiar. It seems far more familiar to try to work it out on the usual human basis, "I'll struggle with the human factors, either inside me or in my world, and make the best of it." What does it look like from the other side of things? We have regained *vertical memory* when we remember that who we are is already present in the field of universal consciousness. We remember another reality, not separate from the one that we're living, not unrelated to this world. We find that part of us is living in a reality of eternal peace and radiance, eternal perfection, and wholeness. There is part of us that has always lived there and has never left.

When you invoke vertical memory, your life changes. You begin to be in position, with others who have had the same experience, to offer something critical in our world today—a radically different paradigm of consciousness, an evolution of consciousness. Not something that is only a slow, step-by-step movement forward, but a great leap into a new experience. It takes courage to take that leap.

Entertain this thought, and see what happens in your awareness and in your personal energy field. Share this thought with other people, and notice how the energy between you shifts.

What if, before we were born, you and I lived together in the realms of universal consciousness? What if, from that eternal place of perfect wholeness, we chose to incarnate together so that we could be spiritual pioneers for humanity now?

Perhaps part of us never left that place of universal consciousness. Part of us is together there, even now, in perfect love, with full agreement and total willingness to do what is ours to do together now.

We are now remembering that eternal reality, that heavenly home, in our experience on Earth. In that spirit, I speak these words to you:

Welcome home. I love you. I serve with you. I remember.

Praise to the Queen of Heaven and Earth

Praise to the Queen of heaven and earth;
She in whom all things are conceived, born, and nourished;
All the creatures who walk on the ground,
The fox, the deer, the ants, and all,
All the birds of the air and the fish of the sea,
The sparrow, the cockatiel, and the salmon,
The fierce hawk, the gentle dove, and all;
She in whom the grass grows,
And in whom the apple tree, which gives its fruit, is nourished;
She who receives the lily petals, when they fall from their stems,
And who receives the baby's tears,
Who hears the prayers of the poor and the rich alike,
And who receives all as her own.

Praise to the Queen of heaven and earth.
Our hearts are carried to you on the wings of our songs,
And in our labors of love,
Sanctified in your rich heart which is our own,
In your work of love which we carry out in our days,
Carrying your blessing
As a kiss on our forehead,

As violets in our hair,
As a golden locket over our heart
Reminding us of how precious you are.

Praise to the Queen of heaven and earth.
You walk among us in our children,
In our closest friends, and friends unknown;
In our lovers,
And as our mothers,
In those who know you and serve you above all else,
And in ourselves,
Shining as bright as the noonday sun,
Or hidden like the sliver moon behind a cloud,
You walk among us as we have eyes to see.

Praise to the Queen of heaven and earth.
All is given to you.
All lives in thee.

Reflections

This is the last chapter of *Becoming a Sun*. It is the last chapter that appears in the book, but it is also the last chapter in my writing process. Throughout the book, I have chosen to tell parts of my personal story, believing that it would ground ideas and awareness in my own life experience. Truthfully, my personal story is through every section of the book—in all the poetry and in all the prose too.

In this moment, I feel as though I have written my memoir. The book has compelled me to reflect on what I have learned and how I learned it. It has caused me to reflect on the seeds of grace I have received from others—from my parents and from amazing friends, mentors, leaders, and teachers—and from life itself. The knowing of grace is the culmination of any creative process, so it is natural that I should be feeling that now.

I see, in a deeper way, how that grace has been with me all along— through my life and through my writing. In this book, I have shared some of the ecstatic joy I have known, and also the challenge and even agony that has been part of my journey. And there was grace through it all.

I have done many things, and I have lived and traveled in many places. Since the year 2000, I have lived at Sunrise Ranch, the spiritual community I lead in Loveland, Colorado. I haven't seen the Northern Lights since that summer in Maine when I was 17. And unfortunately, it has been several years since I have had the opportunity to go skinny-dipping. But I am thrilled to live in a place that is deeply committed to being a teaching and demonstration site for creating a new world. That is the mission of Sunrise Ranch.

At 65 years old, I feel like I've already lived a lifetime and I am ready to live another. I am grandfather to Xavi, a wonderful five-year-old. There is a new generation of inspired, passionate teachers and leaders emerging all around me, and I have the privilege of traveling and offering seminars that accelerate spiritual awakening and deepen the experience of grace. I believe that these experiences, spreading through people, are the hope for our world.

And as I complete this book-writing process, I remember that it is common for people to feel loss, emptiness, regret, and even grief at the end of a creative cycle. Questions arise. *Was it worth it? Why did it go that way? After everything I've done, why don't I have more to show for it? Is there anything good coming after this? Is it all over?*

But looking back, I can well say: *It has been good.* And not only that. *It is good.*

This is grace . . . knowing that the creative process is good—all of it. I am not trivializing the challenges, for me or anyone else. Some of the events along my path have been horrific. And I have lived a relatively charmed life. So many people have it so much worse.

Still, grace holds it all.

I believe that when the seeds of grace grow in people, they have the opportunity to come to know grace in every phase of the creative process. The more they know that grace, the more they radiate that grace to others. Yes, those seeds are already present on the inside for everyone. But it makes a great difference when a human being sows the seeds of grace in someone else. I have unspeakable appreciation for the people who did that for me. The reflections of their light and warmth have, over time, nurtured the emergence of my own sun.

Grace is knowing that all things are evolving to manifest the glory of Being. It comes from seeing life from the perspective of Being, not from the perspective of all the things that are evolving. It is born from someone who is being a sun. A sun radiates grace.

With the conclusion of this book, I am ready to begin a new life. I am ready to invest the seeds of grace in this world. I invite you to do so with me.

We are becoming a sun.

About
David Karchere

David Karchere is an author, speaker and workshop leader, and foremost thought leader on *Primal Spirituality* worldwide. David describes *Primal Spirituality* as our first spirituality—the spirituality we were born with, and the innate, sacred bond that is behind all the world's great religions and spiritual paths.

He developed the *Full Self Emergence* program, a six-month internship for personal development and transformation. David originated the *Healing Chant Workshop* and the *Journey Into the Fire Intensive*. He has offered workshops, trainings and lectures in the United States, Canada, Europe, South Africa, Japan, South Korea and Australia.

David is the spiritual director at Sunrise Ranch, a teaching and demonstration site for *Primal Spirituality*. It is located in Loveland, Colorado, on 350 acres in the foothills of the Rocky Mountains. Sunrise Ranch is staffed by a multigenerational community of 100 people. It is a conference and retreat center and a working farm practicing regenerative agriculture. Founded in 1945, it is the oldest intentional community in the United States.

David is a member of the Evolutionary Leaders Circle.

A Special Invitation From the Author

As a reader of *Becoming a Sun,* I invite you to visit my website, davidkarchere.com, and stay in touch. You can find a calendar of my upcoming events. You can sign up for my newsletter and read about some of my most current thinking.

I'd also like to offer a special invitation to attend my *Becoming a Sun* workshop. I can promise you the opportunity for a transforming and uplifting experience that will change your life. And as a reader of *Becoming a Sun,* I want to offer you a 20% discount on the workshop. You can find the next holding of the workshop on my website. Simply put in the code BASReader as you register to receive the discount.

Made in the USA
Columbia, SC
06 October 2024

43143915R00180